REVELATIONS

REVELATIONS
Essays on Striptease and Sexuality

Margaret Dragu
A.S.A. Harrison

Nightwood Editions
London, Ontario

ISBN 0-88971-117-8
Published in Canada by Nightwood Editions, Box 1426, Station A, London, Ontario N6A 5M2
(Nightwood Editions is a division of blewointmentpress ltd.)

Published with the assistance of the Canada Council and the Ontario Arts Council under their block grant programs. The authors also wish to acknowledge the OAC Writers' Reserve Program for its assistance in the final stages of this project.
Typeset by Ana Coutinho.
Design, layout and collages by Maureen Cochrane.
Printed in Canada by Gagné Printing Ltd.
Photo credits:
Photograph of M. Dragu on cover & page 85 by Barbara E. Wilde.
Photographs on page 13 and 41 by Roger-Viollet.
Photo page 109 courtesy of *Mother Jones* magazine.
Photo page 125 by Maureen Cochrane.

Canadian Cataloguing in Publication Data

Dragu, Margaret
Revelations: essays on striptease and sexuality

Bibliography: p.
ISBN 0-88971-117-8

1. Strip-tease. 2. Sex. I. Harrison, A.S.A.
II. Title.

PN1949.S7D73 1988 792.7'028 C88-095307-1

Table of Contents

Acknowledgements

We wish to express our appreciation to the following: the Canada Council Explorations Program for financial assistance; Colin Campbell, Kristine Dahl, Laurel Dean, Louise Dennys, Peggy Gale, Eldon Garnet, Susan Swan, and Rodney Werden for encouragement and moral support; René Blouin, Mary Canary, Kate Craig, Jane Ellison, Bruce Ferguson, Martha Fleming, and the Glassbourgs for research contacts and places to sleep; James Dubro, Robert Olivier and Centre documentation de La presse, and Michael Walsh for research assistance; Marie-Hélène Fontaine for translations of French-language newspaper articles; David Johnston and Peter Livingston for business assistance; John Massey for inspiration, validation, and substantial help with research; Martin Peterson for the use of Gandalf's Quadex; Diane Scally for identifying these chapters as essays; Carolyn Wood for helping us to find a public context for the manuscript; and all those who gave us interviews.

Margaret Dragu
A.S.A. Harrison

Preface

Canada has the best striptease in the world. Striptease thrives in Canada's major cities and small towns alike, and has not so far given way to more explicit sex shows or token performances as a draw for liquor hustles. Stripping is a cultural product of importance, and its continuing popularity throughout much of North America and parts of Europe indicates that, in terms of sexual entertainment, we westerners have not become total philistines, devoted exclusively to the worship of genitalia and their more obvious functions. For in this utilitarian world, stripping is in a class by itself. It is the only sexual theatre we have that is dedicated to enticement and the arousal of desire as opposed to bald displays of fornication. Striptease is our one shrine to sexual feeling and the enjoyment and celebration of sexual feeling for its own sake.

Margaret Dragu and I wanted to write a book that would reveal the unique nature and merits of stripping, and at the same time address the moral and political issues that cling to sexual entertainment. We focused on two areas of research. A collection of hundreds of newspaper and magazine reports of striptease, dating from the twenties to the present, has revealed the phenomenal intolerance of women's sexuality that pervades western culture. And second, our interviews of strippers, customers, policemen, and other related individuals have provided personal views and experiences that set public and media prejudice in high relief. We have also drawn substantially on Dragu's seven-year career as a stripper in Toronto and Montreal. Our setting is mainly Canada, but we have collected material from some American and European cities as well.

In writing these essays, Dragu and I have kept our voices separate. She has provided a stream of stories and description based on research as well as her own experiences. My undertaking has been an interpretation of Dragu's experiences and of our research material. The result is something like a tv documentary, with ongoing clips of managers, agents, cops, girls and customers in various predicaments, supported by a commentary. Our voices are distinguished in the manuscript by typestyle – Dragu's is in italic, mine in roman.

Through working on this book, I have realized that western culture generates a neurotic symbiosis between sex and morals that is wholly out of control. The very fact that we look on stripping with a mixture of ignorance, intolerance and fascination is evidence of our sexual confusion as a culture. Perhaps the most far reaching conclusion I have come to through this study is that if it were possible to dismiss our irrational fear of sex, and see sexuality – in all of its manifestations – without prejudice, the dropping away of social problems would constitute a revolution.

A.S.A. Harrison

This book is for every woman who ever paid the rent with high heels and a g-string.

I

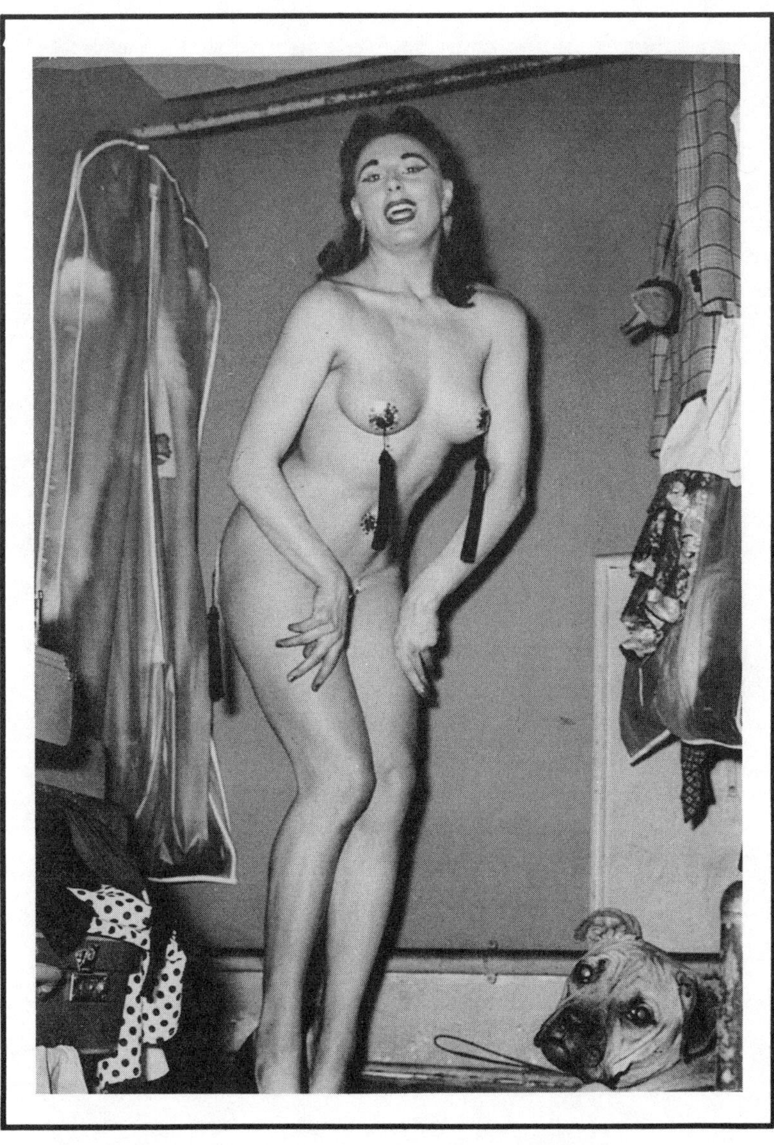

The Striptease Establishment

The strip club is perhaps the only theatre where you can see really good and really terrible performance side by side, with no one making any apparent distinction between the two. This is because strippers are hired less for their performance skills than for good looks and conformism to certain traditions and expectations. But although good dancers are not the rule in strip clubs, you can find a fair number of them there.

Margaret Dragu describes herself as a physically atypical stripper, and claims she succeeded in the business only because she is an exceptional dancer. She landed her first stripping job on that basis. It was at the Copa Cabana – an old-fashioned French Canadian strip club in Montreal. The other girls were petit French Canadians with perfectly proportioned bodies, while Dragu was tall, slightly overweight and strong featured. Although the rule of the house was that all strippers wear pantyhose, which they rolled down and tucked up to fit underneath their g-strings, Dragu was given special exemption because there was no pantyhose long enough for her. She was definitely the exception in the club, admitted only because she could dance.

It is more common, however, to find managers hiring bad performers on the strength of their good looks. Dragu describes a redheaded stripper called Teena, a one-time co-worker, as the worst dancer she's ever seen in her life. She was so awkward, says Dragu, that she used to trip herself on stage, but she was slim and pretty with nice, large breasts. One night Dragu was sitting at the bar watching Teena do her show when the manager sat down beside her and said: "She's so terrible. But she's kinda cute."

The conventionally sexy qualities of blondeness and a big bosom are highly prized in strippers. Dragu recalls working with blonde and buxom Cynthia, who one night had the audience chanting her name in a frenzy of tits-and-blondeness worship. Then there was Arlene, a short girl with enormous breasts that seemed all the larger on her small frame. One night when Arlene bared her monuments, the entire audience stood up and moved a few steps toward the stage in a single, wavelike motion. "If we were a ship, we would have capsized," says Dragu.

But although there is emphasis on physical attributes, each club has its own standards for these, based on the personal taste of the manager. Bridget, who is an attractive redhead, was fired from Toronto's Up Front club because she had a slight pot belly. The lady manager made it clear that this was the issue by cattily asking Bridget if she was pregnant. This particular club favours the slender, flat-bellied and tight-skinned body of the jockette.

Ondine was a Montreal stripper who auditioned for a job and was not hired because the manager didn't think she was attractive. Ondine discovered this by peeking at the manager's private list of girls while waiting in his office, and finding that he had written the words "not pretty" beside her name. But Ondine got a job at another club where the manager liked her well enough to take her on permanently. An interesting sequel to this story is that Ondine was subsequently approached by some people who wanted to photograph her legs for a book about Quebec working women. She appeared in the book as the "Legs of Quebec." Nobody seemed to mind that she was an American from New York.

Some managers give very little consideration to looks or talent and just take whatever comes their way. Dragu tells a story about a club deep in the Quebec countryside where all the waitresses took turns dancing topless. One extremely fat and surly waitress kept skipping her turn until the manager insisted that she dance. He said that everyone must do the same job. She got up on stage, pulled off her dress, and pitched herself angrily from side to side in her panties. The manager seemed satisfied.

Dragu knew one manager who was very fussy at times, and at other times hired anyone who came in. Dragu thinks the occasional duds he hired were his way of keeping the regular girls in line – so they wouldn't begin to think they were indispensable.

More important than either looks or ability is the unexpected standard that strippers perform with ladylike decorum. This means a sense of modesty, and the observance of certain feminine traditions, such as cleanliness and hairlessness. These demands come as much from strippers themselves as from managers and customers. Dragu was once fired for the accident of having her tampax string showing during a performance. It was the other girls who reported her to the manager and urged him to get rid of her. Greta was once fired because she had dirty feet. The girls put a bar of soap on her waitress tray as a hint, but she didn't catch on, so they pressured the manager to fire her. When Dragu was a novice, an older ex-stripper advised her to keep her legs together when doing bumps and grinds because it was more ladylike that way.

The demand that strippers be ladylike exists as a kind of counterpoint to an ever present expectation that they are going to do something gross. It is common to hear a customer praising a particular stripper for being a lady. What he means is that she isn't as much of a whore as you would expect a stripper to be, and that she behaves with more decency than other strippers.

Dragu has received many inverted compliments of this kind, perhaps because she always followed the older ex-stripper's advice and kept her legs together whenever possible. A regular customer once approached her at the Zanzibar in Toronto, after watching her dance for several weeks, to shake her hand and tell her that he liked her because she "took care of business without being a pig."

At that time, the Zanzibar had a swing, operated by hydraulic lift, which the strippers used as a circus-style prop. One night, Dragu was coming down from the heights and the bouncer came along to steady the swing and take her hand as she stepped off. Just before her feet touched the ground, Dragu swept her arm theatrically through the five ballet positions, and as she took the bouncer's hand and stood up, she threw her leg balletically into the air. This was intended as a joke, based on the style of curtain call given at ballet performances. Dragu thought it was a hysterically funny stunt to pull in a strip club. But afterwards, the bouncer said to her: "I wish you could teach all the girls to do that because it's so classy and ladylike."

It is hard to pull off jokes of that kind in strip clubs. Ladylike behaviour puts people at ease because it helps to compensate for the dirty business of sex. But because everybody is half expecting strippers to do something offensive, it is also difficult to pull off a joke based on crudeness. Fonda Peters did it by being as overt as possible. She chewed gum, made armfarts and pointed to her armpit and leg hair, asking the guys if they thought she was a lady. Dragu describes a stripper, who removed her over-the-elbow gloves, finger by finger with her teeth, giving every finger a blow job. She pulled off the joke, says Dragu, by being excessively postured and exaggerated.

Transvestite stripper Iris Rose used to do a classic burlesque act that was charming and ladylike. But one night when the audience was rowdy and insulting, Iris decided to do a different kind of show. First she performed cunnilingus on her armpit. Then she took out a powder puff with a long, gold handle – a prop she normally used to daintily dust her cleavage. This time, however, she stuck the puff down the front of her g-string and pounded it against her crotch until powder came billowing out. Dragu didn't know what to make of this show until Iris came off stage and said: "Well girl, that's my comedy act." Iris had done it as a kind of satire, to match the uncouth behaviour of the men in the audience that night, but of course they didn't get the joke.

The standards for strippers are haphazard and easily give way to the personal tastes and politics of managers, and the whims of strippers. Stripping is a maverick industry in which everyone tends to do whatever he or she thinks best at the time. Meanwhile, the general public is so mesmerized by sexuality per se that managers and strippers are both susceptible to the idea that if the stripper gets her clothes off, little else matters. The result is that stripping is uneven in quality. When you go into a strip club, you never know what you will get.

There is a theory in circulation that stripping is not as good as it once was. I first heard this expressed by Dragu, who told me how stripping in Montreal had passed through various stages of decline – one just before Expo '67, another at the start of the gang warfare in the seventies, and another during the Olympics in 1976. Dragu had picked up this theory from the older strippers and the aging doormen and bartenders she met in clubs. But her most particular source, it turned out, was the woman who sold her g-strings at Johnny Brown theatrical supplies – a woman who said with unquestionable authority: "You should have seen this town before Expo '67."

The Decline Theory seemed reasonable, and I only began to doubt it after hearing a number of different versions that didn't quite add up. Each person's version, I found, had a strong flavour of nostalgia for the good old days when he or she was just starting out in the business.

Ann Corio, an American burlesque queen of the thirties, was horrified by the luridness of sixties strippers. She saw stripping in her own day as a kind of Elysian romp, all innocence and good fun.

Fifties stripper Josephine, who worked in Montreal, began to complain towards the end of her career that stripping had deteriorated in her time. Strippers had forsaken all art and tease, she believed, and now did nothing more than file across the stage with vacuous smiles on their faces, peeling off a few wisps of garments.

Fonda Peters says much the same thing, complaining that there's no art or tease anymore, and that strippers used to be voluptuous and full of fun, but have become toylike and vacuous. But Fonda thinks the decline happened between the mid seventies when she first started stripping and 1980 when she quit.

Journalists corroborate a decline in stripping, but again, there is no consensus about when it happened. Many write vaguely about "today's" strippers not having what it takes. Aging newspaper men have a tendency to wander into some strip joint once every five years and compare the experience unfavourably with their patchy memory of the time before. The fact is that journalists have been complaining that stripping is in a state of decline practically since its beginnings in the late twenties.

Stripping is not, on the whole, any better or worse than it has ever been. But because there are good and bad strippers working together, it is easy to see stripping as all good or all bad, depending on your predisposition.

People who have become disillusioned with stripping are probably among those who were unrealistically enchanted by it in the first place – when they were starry-eyed novice strippers or, in the case of journalists, when they were younger and less jaded.

It is true that really good strippers and people who thoroughly enjoy watching them tend to glorify what is going on in the strip theatre. Their vision of sexual entertainment transcends the establishment concerns with appearance and decorum. These are the few, but they persist. Stripping is surprisingly conservative for a business that exists outside correct society and politics, yet in spite of its conformist ideas about itself and sexuality, it has always been able to make room for visionaries.

II

THE FABULOUS FORUM presents
12, av. george V 75008 paris
tel. 723.32.32
CLUB 1950
DANSEUSES NUES
DANSE CONTINUELLE
Du lundi au dimanche de 11.00 AM à 3.00 PM
happy crazy '85
PARADIS LATIN
S CÉLÈBRE
DU MONDE
CRAZY HORSE
lle
de loin la
PANACHE
NOUVELLE REVUE
LIDO
iner dansant
gne et Revue 440 F
0 h 15
gne et Revue 300 F
COMPRIS
RVATIONS 563 11 61 ET AGENCES
Bal du Moulin Rouge
20 h. Dîner dansant Champagne et Revue 440 F
22 h et 0 h Champagne et Revue 300 F
PRIX NETS SERVICE COMPRIS
femmes, femmes, femmes...
MONTMARTRE PLACE BLANCHE 606 00 19 ET AGENCES

Consumers' Guide to Strippers

Nightclubs are extremely politicized organizations. The power dramas that are played out in the modern world internationally, nationally, regionally and locally are all happening in miniature inside each club. Everyone is there: the conservatives, liberals, fascists, communists, imperialists, socialists, radicals, terrorists, laborites, unionists, feminists, right-to-lifers, back-to-the-landers, anarchists, welfare recipients, illegal immigrants, do-gooders, ne'er do wells, rounders, scoundrels, criminals and junkies, doctor, lawyer and indian chief....

Both onstage and off there is a complete range of right wing, left wing, mid wing and wingless views on the art and business of stripping. No two people can agree. Some think stripping is showbiz, some think it is a sexual service, some strippers are soft, pink, baby-doll types, and some are pistol-toting, black-lipped, black-leathered new wavers. Some girls were born backstage on vaudeville trunks and their mama was a carnie stripper and their daddy a ballycaller. Some girls are orphan debutantes who lost the family fortune and would rather be Shakespearean actresses but have fallen to this. Some are saving to go back to school to be physicists, some dream of becoming airline hostesses. Some girls are ashamed of their job and keep it a secret from their families, some girls think of the club as home, and their boyfriends and mom and dad drop in and even on their day off they hang around the club. Some would be disowned if word ever got out. Some are gay, some are straight. Some are wired on cliff-hanging romances. Some are mothers. Some are happy to do their own thing and some want to make others do as they do. Some want to organize to get better working conditions and better pay, while some see themselves as mavericks and want to negotiate their own deals privately. Some never do bumps and grinds, some are politically and spiritually involved in showing their genitals, some would never dream of taking off their high heels, some think stripping is going to the workout gym to improve their rhomboids and trapezoids. Some like customers and even marry customers, some are manhaters, some are jugglers, mime artists and circus folk, some are vegetarians. Members of the second-oldest profession embody every style, taste and belief you can imagine.

To help clarify some of the major differences from one stripper to the next, I have catalogued ten distinct types of stripper.

Burlesque Queen

This type fulfills everyone's idea of a classic, old-time stripper. She possesses trunkloads of vaudeville-style costumes replete with sequins, ostrich plumes, maribu trim, and rhinestone-studded chiffon. She wears long gloves and stockings with garters and is the last purveyor of the classic bump and grind. Her style is in the tradition of Gypsy Rose Lee and all those dames of the thirties. She has survived fashion and the sands of time with true grit. She is a star, preserving showbiz traditions with the resolve of ban-the-bomb protesters. I adore the B.Q. because she has such showmanship.

One of my all-time favourite Burlesque Queens is Pat Lee, known in the business as The Devil-Made-Me-Do-It Girl. I met her at an old strip club called the Gaiety in Miami Beach. The Gaiety is a burlesque palace in the old style – all done up in red velour and velvet trimmed with fringe and gilt braid. The new age has penetrated only in the form of a large video screen that pumps out hard-core pornography.

The night I watched Pat Lee strip, she wore a traditional rhinestone sheath evening gown with matching hat and gloves. Even though the audience never surpassed ten sleepy and morose men, she stopped after every song in her act to strike a burlesque pose and say firmly: "Thank you, thank you." She made those men applaud. She knew she wasn't a videotape – she was a live entertainer, a Queen of Burlesque, dedicated to the preservation of charm and artifice and the Grand Style.

New Wave Stripper

There is always a new wave. In stripping, there is a New Wave stripper who is the anti-traditionalist. She refuses to conform to popular culture's idea of what is sexual – what behaviour, attitude or aesthetic is sexually pleasing, or sexually correct. She is a rule breaker. She defies traditions like her new wave counterparts in new wave music, new wave cinema, new wave architecture, and post modern art and dance. She is the post modern stripper. She is arrogant and angry but also confident and flowing with vitality.

The first New Wave stripper I ever saw was Vanessa, who was dancing at the Silver Dollar on College Street in 1977. She had recently shaved her head, and it had grown back to the downy brushcut stage. She was tall and beautiful, like a fashion model, and wore a black vinyl harness that criss-crossed her torso and left her breasts exposed. She was also wearing high black leather boots with high heels.

Back then, just dressing like that was totally shocking. Vanessa broke enough rules with her style alone – she didn't have to put new wave content into her act. Nowadays, strippers make explicit fascist references. They wear SS insignias or use political music to make specific comments.

I worked with a New Wave stripper called Roz at the Colonial in Toronto. Roz was very blond and striking. Chiselled face – almost Bowie like. She was a writer. She was recovering from a difficult love affair.

Roz dressed in black a lot. Purchased most of her costumes from Courage My Love, a second-hand clothing store, and fixed them up. I remember one find of hers – a black satin flared skirt trimmed in gold brocade. It was so heavy that as she spun in circles it carved a perfect arc around her body. She used tough, noisy music like the new wave classic by The Strangers called "Walkin' Down The Beaches Lookin' At The Peaches," which would make the mild-mannered business patrons at lunchtime look up from their fried chicken wings in confusion. She also used David Bowie's "Beauty And The Beast," choosing her cold, sharp gestures of defiance and her footstomping and spinning to underscore his pointed lyrics. "You can't say no to the beauty and the beast." Another song she used was the Bryan Ferry remake of "These Foolish Things Remind Me Of You" – a borderline song that parodies sentimental feelings, yet through its toughness exposes the raw nerve of pain and loss.

Roz never smiled. She danced angry. She had a modern sexual presence that managers and customers could not understand. Everyone kept telling her to smile. "Smile Roz. You're so pretty. Why don't you smile?" She would tell them to fuck off. She knew she was good and she wasn't about to try to be the pretty-girl-is-just-like-a-melody kind of stripper.

The New Waver wants to annihilate all the things the Burlesque Queen is dedicated to preserving. But as fast as she is smashing traditional aesthetics, she is presenting new ones. Anti-gracefulness and anti-beauty veer to an obsession with a signature sneer. The sneer becomes a new icon, along with the power symbols and insignia. Ban the baby dolls and don the Ilsa-the-She-Wolf-of-the-SS uniform. Ultimately, the radically opposed camps of the Burlesque Queen and the New Wave stripper meet in an obsession with fetishistic symbols and props. Opposite camps meet at the icon supermarket.

Vamp

According to Webster's, a vamp is a woman who uses her charms and wiles to seduce or exploit men. In popular culture, a vamp is one of the female archetypes. Theda Bara and the women in Conan Comix are vamps. They are hot, sexy, sophisticated and very much in control. A vamp has knowledge in her eyes. She knows a thousand and one things about the land of desire. She is not a slut, regardless of the number of lovers, admirers and followers who dangle from her string. She knows what she wants and she gets it on her terms.

How can you tell you might be in the presence of a Vamp stripper? She often wears classic evening gowns and long gloves, but she is completely different from the Burlesque Queen. The B.Q. is all brassy trumpet and cheap rimshot showbiz backbeat. The Vamp is tasteful sax jazz – all hot and cool. She may stray into the s&m dominatrix or Wicked Wanda cat woman persona, but she never falls into the kind of fetishism exhibited by the New Waver. She can be earthy too, like the vamps who appear as Amazon Warriors and occasionally vampires. Quebec is fond of vampire acts.

The first genuine Vamp stripper I ever encountered was Miss Nude Earth. She had olive skin, large breasts and black hair that fell below her waist. She could mesmerize the Robert Bar Salon. She did a vampire act complete with black light on billowing white negligee, a coffin and fake blood! You could see in her eyes that she was a Vamp. She had burning, knowledgeable, almost catlike eyes. She also did a catwoman act in a tiger skin with a whip and stiletto heel shoes.

Nadine is a slightly cooler and more modern version of the Vamp. I first saw her in a film about striptease. She wore a diaphanous dress, and had her hair cut short and straight. She looked like Cleopatra. She spun and turned on a set that was filled with vapour. I felt that unmistakeable feeling I always have around a Vamp – it is an honour to be in her presence, an honour to look at her.

A.S.A. and I finally caught up with Nadine in the flesh at Stage 212, where she danced in a French-cut satin corset. She was so calm and cool, not desperate to get our attention or approval. We saw her again at the Latin Quarter in the suburbs, wearing a red and black aerobic outfit and looking very swank high fashion. When I chatted with her between sets, she said she was having a big party to celebrate her tenth year in the business.

I saw her after that at Gimlet's downtown, still wearing the high-cut aerobic panties, but dancing to a song by Patti Smith that had a long bagpipe solo in it that wailed and wailed in ever-increasing decibels. The ceiling was so low over the stage that her head almost touched it as she spun and turned, using her arms to carve intersecting arcs with her head. She was riveting. It was like watching an ancient ritual performed by a high priestess.

Dingbat Artist

Dingbat Artists are loners. Often they are painters, writers, dancers or photographers, who strip as a way of making money. Their aesthetic is totally individual and is reflected in their stripping performances. They often appear misplaced in strip clubs because they just cannot manage to follow the rules. But Dingbat Artists have a long tradition of working strip clubs – a bohemian tradition that has always linked the worlds of the stripper and the artist.

These strippers are not bent on smashing traditions because they do not take tradition seriously, if they notice it at all. Instead, the eclectic and totally individual Dingbat Artist ignores tradition and just does her own thing. Dingbats don't usually last long in stripping – it is too conservative for them and they are always getting fired.

Eva was almost six feet tall and incredibly beautiful. She had been a high-fashion model since she was fifteen. She was a writer and an artist and a bohemian. She was so gorgeous that men would brake their cars to a screeching halt and back up to take another look at her as she walked down the street. Their jaws fell open and they stared and stared. I am talking genuine gorgeous.

When I first met Eva she had shaved her head and was wearing a fur hat 24 hours a day to get past the brushcut stage. I think she first got the idea of trying her hand at stripping when she came to see me at the Copa. She had been silkscreening, and arrived at the club looking absolutely gorgeous but with one hand and forearm painted green. The doorman let her in and then came over to tell me: "Your friend is here to see you. She's beautiful, but what's wrong with her arm?" I guess he thought it was some dreadful skin disease.

The Copa had such a low ceiling that I could barely fit under it with low heels, so when Eva decided to strip she started at the Robert Bar Salon. We became roommates in a huge loft on St. Laurent. We had trunkloads of clothes and fabric and fringe that we pinned on ourselves with costume jewellery before hitting the streets of Montreal. We had fun. Eva always had more guts than me.

She made her stripping debut in a monkey mask. Our mutual agent, Don d'Amico asked me why Eva wanted to hide her beauty by wearing a mask. He didn't understand her visual theatrics at all. She did a vampire act complete with teeth that she revealed at a climactic point in the music, often making people scream. She danced with spiders pinned all over her. She stuck glitter to one side of her jaw so it looked like she was spewing it from her mouth. She once stripped as the spirit of the city of Montreal in yarn, fabric and rocks. Another time, she stripped in a costume of feathers – not boas and the usual stripper stuff, but real bird feathers, all gorgeously soft, brown and flecked. She danced as a trapped wild bird.

Having been an actress, she also leaned to the dramatic in her acts. She pretended the shoe she removed was bewitched and was casting a spell on her. She made the shoe chase her around the stage, holding it in one hand over her head, shaking it as if it was the thing in control. Then she wrenched herself away from it, throwing it down and gasping for air.

The audience was always totally stunned by her shows, but managers were divided in their opinions of her. Sometimes she was fired but every now and then she was held over. She was a terrific entertainer, and so beautiful. She didn't last long – a year at most. She was always slightly ashamed of stripping I think. Now she is married to a rich businessman and doesn't want people to know about her stripping past. The last time I saw her, after a long interval, she was as beautiful as ever and driving around in an expensive sports car, money worries far behind. One of the first questions she asked me was "You aren't still in clubs, are you Dragu?" She was so relieved that I was not.

Another Dingbat Artist was Greta, who was a painter, a writer and an artist's model. Greta looked like Little Orphan Annie – curly hair and a genuine little girl feeling. She was pale with open eyes and an open face. She was often depressed and a little crazy. She had beautiful breasts – a surprise on her childlike body.

Greta danced at the Colonial in Montreal once. She wore voluminous rags all tied about her body. This costume was accessorized with loads of glitter on her skin and topped off with a 1920s straw boater hat. She spun and danced and leapt up into the air and then froze for a bar of music or two and then hurled herself around again. Her spinning rag dress was a deep, bizarre image. She was fired by Dino before the week was out. He said: "We pay you to strip, not to express yourself in creative dance."

Undaunted, Greta got a gig at Le Relais. There she did an act in harem pants and a gauzy top. She removed her top layers, then took off her harem pants to reveal that instead of a g-string, she was wearing a pair of men's jockey shorts. And not only that, there was a noticeable bulge in those shorts. After another song or two, during which the audience must have been wondering if she was man, woman, hermaphrodite or just what, Greta stuck her hand down her jockey shorts and took out a huge bottle of glitter which she sprinkled over the audience. Everyone laughed. They adored Greta. Art makes a hit. But the management didn't buy it. She could stay the rest of the week – but she couldn't do the jockey shorts routine. All the girls had to wear a g-string.

The classic Dingbat Artist stripper has to be Sylvie. She always had a million scams and schemes that never quite came to fruition – from buying the Waverley Hotel – home of the Silver Dollar Strip Club – to doing an interview series on stripping for radio. She loved to get into trouble, and was proud of the trouble she managed to get into. She was a vivacious performer, with a knockout perfect body that didn't quite match her face, and possibly that was what made her special – more than pretty. She had a bit of the Edith Piaf little sparrow look – huge glasses and sharp little nose and chin, yet not sad like Piaf.

She told me about working a club in the burbs and running into a motorcycle gang in the parking lot after her shift. She would tell me these scary stories and laugh. I have a strong image of Sylvie laughing despite everything. I could never tell if the stories were true or not. I feared there was a bit of the Boy Who Cried Wolf about Sylvie. She lived in a grey zone between reality and imagination, and I thought she might get into real trouble some day, and nobody would believe her – maybe not me either.

I ran into Sylvie at Daddy's Money in Yorkville, where I was working as a feature. One Monday night I came in and there was Sylvie dancing on stage. She was dressed in an elegant, short, black cocktail dress and high heels. Her hair was hennaed. She looked like a million bucks. When she saw me she waved and threw her head back and laughed right out loud.

I watched her dance. She was beautiful. But my strongest thought was that she wasn't going to last, because even though she was a good dancer and performer, she didn't believe in stripping. It was a gag and fast money and a fast experience. She didn't understand the nuances.

Much later Sylvie told me she preferred stripping for friends at parties. And she liked doing stags, she said. She did a stag once with another Dingbat Artist stripper called Tia Maria, a short, petite, dark-haired writer who was known in clubs for dancing to Bob Dylan and doing Martha Graham exercises and getting sent home for dressing in a costume of safety pins and flour sacking painted with graffiti. Tia Maria says that she and Sylvie barely got out of the hotel room alive the night of the stag, since the men were sure they were hookers, rather than strippers. Tia Maria never stagged again. But Sylvie could handle the fast and scary lane and even preferred it.

Dingbat Artist strippers are elitist and esoteric in their singular vision of the world, which they bring whole to the strip stage. They are not fighting popular values like the New Waver – they are oblivious to them as they communicate in their private vocabulary of gesture and symbol.

Hippie Stripper

I admit that I am an aging hippie. I eat brown rice and tofu and want to do something about environmental abuse and world peace. But I was never a Hippie stripper. These girls are earnest and pragmatic, with a disdain for artifice, including makeup, perfume, high heels and stockings. They usually have armpit and leg hair, and often they have long hippie tresses on their heads too. They believe nudity is healthy – not exotic. Taking off their clothes means very little to them since they swim and sunbathe and do yoga in the nude anyway. They aren't ashamed of their bodies and they don't equate nudity with sexuality, so they don't project sexuality when they strip. Instead, they radiate health and serenity. Often they are self-absorbed while on stage, involved in their own meditative experience rather than in a communication with the audience.

Jamie was a Hippie stripper. She was a competitive diver and swimmer in her adolescence, then turned to modern dance, and eventually took a job stripping at Gary Taylor's in Vancouver. Jamie used to go to work in a cotton sundress. Her act consisted of getting up on stage, taking off her sundress, doing yoga in her cotton panties, then lying down for her floor show which featured something she refers to as her "crisis" which was a kind of fake orgasm. Then she put her clothes back on and went to the park to sunbathe between sets.

While taking Jamie's dance classes in Vancouver, I met another Hippie stripper called Karen, who lived in the country and worked at No. Five Orange. Karen had long blonde hair and a slim dancer's body. She looked upon stripping at No. Five as a gym workout. The club encouraged this aesthetic by installing rings and hooks and bars on the ceiling so the girls could do their gymnastic stunts. When Karen stripped, she didn't make any contact with the audience. She danced her first song in a leotard decorated with a few accessories such as a jazz skirt, understated jewellery and velcroed bits of fabric that she could whip off. After dispensing with everything but the leotard, she leapt up to the rings and bars and worked on her reps (body builder talk for repetitions of sets of strengthening exercises). She moved well and looked good, but she was like moving wallpaper. You could glance up from your beer and see her in various stages of her workout, and it was visually lovely but not at all engaging.

Hippie strippers let the customer provide the sexual content. They are totally unaware of the history and tradition of what they are doing. I have a certain fondness for them, but in my heart of hearts, I don't think any stripper should be allowed to take off her high heels.

Greaser Mama

Greaser Mamas are not the real Hell's Angel type of motorcycle girls. Biker mamas are a special underground classification that I've had no personal contact with. But there is a popular culture version of greasers and their mamas. This scene is all blue jeans and cutoff t-shirts and competitive sports and beer. The mamas can drink and drug and party and laugh as loud and long and hard as the guys they hang out with. Greasers respect a mama who can drink them under the table. There is a certain equality between the greasers and the Greaser Mamas.

These girls are usually good looking, with large breasts and small waists. Like the Hippie stripper, they have a wide-open sexuality, but unlike the Hippie they share themselves with the audience. A Greaser Mama can come up to a table of regulars and slap them on the back and say, "So how's it goin, eh?" – even though she is almost naked and wearing five-inch high heels. There is no threat of sexual contact since she usually "belongs" to someone and every-

one knows it, usually because her boyfriend and his buddies are regulars at the club.

The first Greaser Mama I ever worked with was a runaway Jewish American Princess with long black hair like Yvonne de Carlo on the tv series "The Munsters." She had fabulous cheekbones and almond shaped eyes. She was short and full breasted, with a luscious big bum – a real beauty. She danced to Marvin Gaye's "Mercy Mercy Me." She would lazily and langorously throw her head back, tossing her long hair, and then spin and pirouette in a slow ecstatic way as she slowly peeled off her clothes.

Her ex-boyfriend was a real motorcycle gang member. They broke up on good terms. She loved sex, particularly sex with cocaine. She would tell me stories about being so into it – so very very hot and so all-velvety inside. She described taking her lover to her high-rise apartment, turning on the stereo, gluing her mouth to his, and making love all night long. Tooting and making love. I really liked this greaser chick, and I was pleased that she thought I was a good stripper. It meant something coming from her because I thought she understood sex.

I once worked with a beautiful Greaser Mama called Wendy, who had a boyfriend called Jude, who was in jail. Wendy had a tattoo on her arm that said, "Jude's Property." While Jude was in the slammer she was constantly horny and always talking about it. She would come into the dressing room, swaying back and forth like a football player, as Greaser Mamas do since they tend to be anti-graceful, and say, "Yeah, you know, since Jude's been gone I'm horny as hell. I started masturbating with a broomstick handle this morning. Thought I was gonna get splinters."

There was a gang of regulars at the club, and one night I overheard Wendy telling them this very story. I would never tell a gang of guys a story like that without expecting trouble. But Wendy was such a slapper, she got away with it. Their response to her at all times was "What a girl."

Like Hippie Strippers, Greaser Mamas are open and guiltless. But unlike the ascetic Hippies, they are hedonists. They love alcohol, drugs, fast cars and motorcycles.

Sex Kitten

Sex Kittens are coy and manipulative, playing the helpless and passive female but secretly plotting, using pouts and giggles and little-girl tactics to get what they want. The Sex Kitten prances around the stage and shakes herself at the men as if she were saying, "It's not my fault you want to stick it in, I am only six years old, and I've never seen a big hard thing like that, mister. How about an all-day sucker?" It is unbearable.

I worked with a Sex Kitten called Candy at Daddy's Money in Yorkville. Candy was blonde, blue-eyed and perfectly proportioned. She arrived on a Wednesday and didn't sync in with the rest of us girls who had been there since Monday. Candy didn't see herself as part of the team. She cut us out of her reality. She was waitressing between sets and she spent all her time on the floor hustling. She laughed too loudly for an unseen camera, was controlled and calculated, always very focused, always smiling, aware of her every gesture. Her laugh lasted just long enough for some guy to grease her palm with silver.

I couldn't stand her and neither could the other girls, but I have to admit that when she danced, the place stopped breathing. She used hit parade music and wore a jewelled t-bar g-string. Very American. She whipped off her clothes in two seconds and got down to some heavy preening and posing and giggling. She turned upside down and put her head between her legs and gave her Sex Kitten giggle and wave. She romped through the poses of Miss November, Miss March and Miss July. She was pretty athletic and she could really sell it. She scampered around after her set and cleaned up on tips. All the men's eyes were glued on Candy as she minced about to get their offerings. She probably made as much tip money in one night as the other waitresses made in a week. You had to hand it to her – the walking, talking, giggling cash register.

Candy was crass, yet the guys adored her. It bugged me that she was rewarded by the customers when she was so oblivious to the religion of stripping. I wanted to punch her in the kisser.

Tipoffs that you are in the presence of a Sex Kitten: maribu trimmed baby-doll pajamas, pouts, giggles, a slightly arched back and a "golly-gosh-gee-whiz" sensibility.

Pathetic Waif

While the Sex Kitten poses as helpless and docile, the Pathetic Waif really is helpless and docile. The Waifs break my heart and fascinate me at the same time. Watching them strip is like watching a freak show at the circus. They are as riveting as a traffic accident in progress.

Pathetic Waifs are the junkies, the lost souls and the hopeless wrecks of the strip scene. They are the stripper with the three kids and the husband with the bad back. They are the stripper married to the creepy, jealous guy who takes all their money and beats them. They are the stripper who finds a sleazy pimp and hooks on the side. They are sad and have no spirit and are victims with no control over their very sad lives. When A.S.A. called the Vice Squad in Toronto to ask about nudity and obscenity laws, the officer with the Scottish accent informed her that all strippers were "pathetic." Much of the civilian world thinks of strippers only in these terms.

Natasha was a ballet dancer who started stripping because she was too fat for ballet. Not fat by strip standards – just too fat for The National Ballet of Canada. I met her at the Robert Bar Salon where she danced to terrific jazz and blues music. She was a junkie. She moved like she was going through molasses. Sometimes it took her one whole song to peel off one silver glove. It wasn't uncommon for Natasha to finish her music tape and still have half her costume on. We would have to quickly put on another tape – any old tape – to give her enough time to get the rest of her clothes off and get off the stage. Then the rest of the night's schedule would be off.

In the dressing room, Natasha would scuff around in a pink chenille bathrobe, fuzzy old slippers and hair rollers. She would float and melt around the furniture like a junkie housewife. Natasha needed lots of time to get ready for her act. Sometimes it took her ten minutes just to stand up.

I knew her ex boyfriend who made her music tapes. He said she was beautiful and sexy, but pathetic. He claimed she was very horny when on smack. He sometimes made heroin puns in the music he selected for her, using jazz titles like Horse Silver and other famous heroin songs for her repertoire. It was an inside joke.

When I took my dance class of artists on a tour of Toronto strip clubs in 1975, we went to Starvin Marvin's, where we saw a stripper who moved like she was in a hypnotic trance. She was very slow and very erotic. She had bad skin and I assumed she was a junkie. The hypnotic, floating dance and the bad skin are tipoffs. The skin comes from the diet of three chocolate bars between each set that often goes with the junkie lifestyle.

There are Pathetic Waifs who are not junkies. They are victims in other ways. They feel like a black hole in space and you can tell that they hate to be at the club doing what they are doing. Like blonde Annette from Timmins who was deaf in one ear and had to do double shifts because she was supporting her young daughter – the only joy in her life – and her layabout husband who disapproved of her working as a stripper. Annette had weeks when she would do nothing but cry between sets. Then there was the skinny Quebecois stripper I worked with who danced to only one song on the jukebox: "Season in the Sun." She was all bones and dark eyes with long, straight, limp brown hair. She wore Woolworth's bikini panties and no makeup. She gave no effort and no energy to her work. Her eyes were glazed over as she swayed lightly to the music, looking past the men in the audience, meditating on her hopeless existence.

You can see Pathetic Waifs in other jobs besides stripping. I have worked with them in factories and coffee shops. They all have the same "I don't want to be here but I don't know what to do about it" look.

Jockette

The Jockette is the essence of popular culture. She is the perfect version of whatever body men are buying this year, and she radiates the status quo. She has a wholesome, and even a virginal air about her, so it can be a shock to find her taking off her clothes in a strip club. She evokes a lot of desire, but she also evokes anger – from women who are jealous of her beauty, and from men who know that she wouldn't give them the time of day.

Being so wholesome and well-adjusted, Jockettes often take part in athletics. They ski, run, sail or windsurf. They have no imagination, but merely reflect the ideas, politics, fashions, and sexual ideals of the moment. The women you see in beer commercials are often this type. They are graceful and pretty, but boring because they have no point of view and nothing to say. Most Jockettes drain me of patience, but a few have a pulsing and honest sexuality, and that can make all the difference.

A.S.A. and I saw an unusually wonderful Jockette at Stage 212. She was a dark-haired beauty who wore the Jockette uniform of the moment – satin shorts, leg warmers, high heels and a singlet t-shirt. This very hot Jockette made good use of the boxing-ring style stage at the 212. She slowly crawled on her hands and knees towards one man sitting on one side of the stage. She was totally in control and riveting – a beautiful animal in heat in the ring.

I once worked with a Jockette whose only flaw was slight buck teeth. One night she decided she wanted a new costume, but it was midnight, and nothing was open except Ford Drugs. So she went to Ford Drugs and bought some wide pink ribbon. She sewed a pink bow onto a g-string, and tied pieces of ribbon together to make a very unstable bra. It covered her as long as she didn't move too much. She wore it for one song, and did nothing more than walk slowly and cautiously across the stage, from one side to the other. So tedious, and yet the audience was riveted, waiting breathlessly the whole time for a piece of ribbon to flap up and reveal a glimpse of one of her forbidden, girl-next-door breasts.

If Jockettes are dull, it's because of what is in their heads. Their middle-class values permeate their acts as well as their lives. Yet they don't have to be good performers because enough men are happy just looking at their perfect bodies and breathing in their status quo personalities.

Intellectual

There are two things I like to see in a stripper. One is the supremely sexual woman who can transfix my very being and make time stand still. This kind of stripper can belong to any category. The other is a thinker who puts her view of life into her act. The Intellectual stripper is political and she is a philosopher. Stripping is the forum she uses to express her ideas and values. Her act combines theatre, performance art, dance and cabaret. What makes her different from the New Waver and the Dingbat Artist is that she embraces stripping to make her point rather than fighting it or being unaware of it.

I doubt that Gwendolyn would call herself an Intellectual stripper, but she is more of a thinker than she makes out. She talks tough and she is tough, but she is also smart. Because she has trained in mime, magic and theatre, and because she is experienced in comedy and gymnastics, her acts are sophisticated. She is well known for her little girl act, which is not the usual burlesque schtick of the pouting big girl pretending to be a baby. She is a Victorian raggedy ann doll come to life. She gets close to a real child's sexuality, skipping and bounding around the stage with an anti-graceful joie de vivre.

Gwendolyn is also an activist on the stripping front. The last time I saw her she was doing a standup act at a feminist cabaret for International Women's Day. She knew she would be playing to a house that might be provoked by her way of thinking, her way of living, her values and the material she would present. In fact, the collective at the dress rehearsal wasn't sure whether to let her go on. To their credit, the vote was finally yes, Gwendolyn stays, and she was great. And to the credit of the audience, at least half thought she was funny, good, and saying something important. She is all of those things, but above and beyond those qualities, Gwendolyn has guts.

Fonda Peters wants to challenge peoples' ideas about what is sexy and appealing in women. She likes to do a traditionally sexy come-on, and then turn it around with something from left field. Her repertoire of irreverant acts includes doing armfarts and making fart noises with her mouth, playing with her chewing gum, making faces, squatting, picking her nose, sticking out her tongue, and pointing to her armpit hair. She interacts with her audience, often questioning the men about what they find sexy in women.

Bridget oscillates between Intellectual and Burlesque Queen. She has done an amazing assortment of routines. Once she dressed as a dirty old man flasher, complete with trenchcoat and cigarette. I have seen her perform with hockey socks and feather plumes. She has been Wonder Woman, a Brownie, and a creature from the Rocky Horror Show. But a favourite of mine was a show she did at Le Strip. Bridget was dressed as a Bag Lady, with cigarette butt, ragged clothes, and hair wrapped in a kerchief. She was pushing a small shopping cart in which another stripper was squatting, dressed in cherries, grapes and lettuce held in place with saran wrap – miles of it. The second stripper leapt out of the shopping cart, peeled and ripped off the saran wrap, and fed the fresh fruit and veg to the audience. Perhaps the lettuce was a little wilted by then. The music was a collection of rock and roll songs about food. The act bordered on the sophomoric, but enthusiasm, energy and skill pushed it into the Monty Python meets Gloria Steinem meets Animal House realm. It was funny, conscious and abnormal. The Intellectual stripper challenges the status quo. She is an activist in the realm of sexual values and ideals. She is the stripper who carves new sexual space in the world.

The Jockette and the Intellectual meet in middle-class consumerism. The Jockette is the middle-class sex product, embodying the sexual identity, consciousness and morality of the times without comment or awareness. The Intellectual, on the other hand, offers a discussion of status-quo morality and sexual values.

III

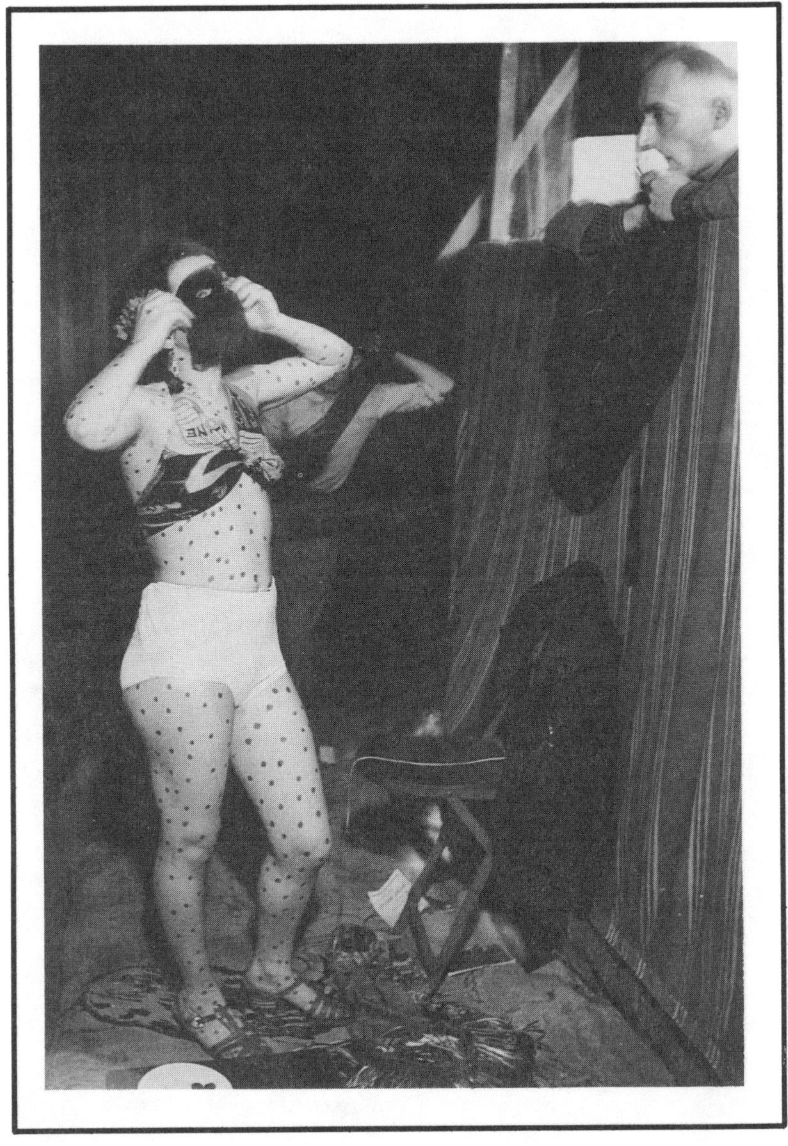

Why Queen Elizabeth Doesn't Strip

It was in September of '79 that I first interviewed Dragu about stripping. At the time, I didn't know what the problems and issues were in the stripping world, and I had not prepared a line of inquiry. For the first hour, Dragu talked about strippers' costumes. The most interesting thing that came up was how much she liked polyester. "It's cheap, it shines, you don't have ironing to worry about, and it's something people can relate to," she told me with energy. I had to laugh. But as we talked on, something began to emerge that seemed important.

Dragu had just quit stripping at the time. Stripping had hurt her, she said, for a number of reasons: bad working conditions, unethical management policies, and abuse from men in the audience. It was audience abuse that seemed to be the biggest sore point. As Dragu talked, her feelings of hostility towards men came into strong relief. I wanted to hear specific stories, and she told me two.

She had been working at the Colonial Tavern on Yonge Street, doubling as a stripper and a waitress. One night, she was waiting on a table of five American businessmen who were in Toronto for a convention. The men all ordered doubles, and she served them a couple of rounds. Dragu was fully dressed, but she had been stripping intermittently.

It was the law in Toronto at the time that strippers keep their g-strings on. These out-of-towners weren't happy with this state of affairs, and kept asking Dragu in loud, rude tones when she and the other strippers were going to take off their g-strings and show their *muffs* (their word). The men mauled her as she served their drinks, and kept offering her money to take off her g-string next time her set came up. Dragu asked them to stop bothering her, and threatened to have them thrown out, but this only made them laugh.

As she arrived at their table with a third round of drinks, Dragu became so angry at the men's continued aggression that she impulsively turned her tray upside down over their table. The drinks poured from the table into their laps, but all they did was laugh drunkenly. The joke was on Dragu. She had lost the money it had cost her to buy the liquor from the bar, and she had not made her point.

"They were so sure," said Dragu, "that if they gave me enough money, the law would change, and that was all I needed to animate my desires. Men think we're all secretly dying to take off our g-strings, and twenty or fifty dollars is gonna do the trick. We're not human to them. We're just windup toys that will do anything for money."

Later in our talk, she said, "Men address strippers in ways that would shock their wives. 'Hey baby, sit on my face,' and 'Come over here, I guess you really want it.' A lot of fantasy about who we are and what our sexual needs are, all of it completely off base."

She told me another story about being grabbed while working at the Zanzibar, up the street from the Colonial. She was dancing on a small, circular stage when a man approached her from behind and put his hand between her thighs. It was terrifying, she said, to be touched suddenly from behind while performing. She left the stage without finishing her set, and a little later someone told her that the manager had dragged the offender into the alley in back of the club and that he had been "taken care of." Dragu's comment on telling me this was, "I don't care how much he was punished, it wasn't enough."

At the time, Dragu's outrage and hostility puzzled me. I didn't feel sympathetic. I thought she was overreacting, and I asked her what she expected. Surely she must realize that being a stripper made her fair game for sexual insults and abuse. And that, of course, was what most people said.

Now, several years of research later, I see my initial attitude as ignorant and unconsidered.

The turning point in my thinking was to realize that women in general are judged by the same standards used for strippers. We live in a society where it is always open season on women who dress or behave in overtly sexual ways. "She was asking for it," is what people say, and what they have been saying for a long time, even in courtrooms. Astonishing as it may seem, sexuality in women is one of the biggest taboos of our civilization. It has been a revelation to me to recognize the manic dimensions of our fear and hatred of sexy women, and to realize that this attitude is so embedded in our way of life that we take it for granted.

I was surprised to discover that the fallen woman is still a viable concept. I supposed that sexuality in women had become acceptable since the liberating changes of the sixties. This is an era, I thought, when women's magazines talk openly about sex, and encourage their readers to have affairs. Most of the women I know have had many lovers. Some of my friends are lesbians, and one or two have worked as prostitutes. Furthermore, all of this is out in the open. It seemed to me that we had finally discarded the stringent virtues prescribed for women in the time of our mothers and grandmothers, whose lives were shaped by the obsessive repression of the Victorian era with its polarized good and bad women.

But as I realized, our sexual code is not based in the mania of a single century, and is not so easily done away with. Christian-Judaic history speaks unremittingly of the corrupt and corrupting female. To discover the age and continuing vitality of the brand, it is only necessary to take a quick look at our language. Most of the words available to describe a woman with a sexual identity are words of slander. *Whore, tart, slut, prostitute, broad, baggage, hosebag* and *douchebag*, for instance. (Some words, such as *courtesan* and *vamp* carry class value or grudging respect.) The slang for female genitalia, namely the word *cunt*, is the worst thing you can call a woman, and implies that a woman uses her sexuality to manipulate. The equivalent for a man is *prick*, an insult without a specifically sexual connotation. To insult a man sexually, it is necessary to call him a *cocksucker*, a *motherfucker*, or some name that describes his sexual activities as perverse according to acceptable standards. The merely promiscuous man is indulged with names like *gigolo, ladies' man*, and even just *bachelor*.

But this is not a state of affairs that is imposed on women by men, and it is not only women who suffer from it. We buy into the myth of women's sexual degeneracy as a whole society, and the sexual role definitions that result put pressure and limitations on all of us, men and women alike. Observe that in cultures where there is greater intolerance of women's sexuality, you also find the most rigidly defined sexual roles.

Given our collective phobia about sexy women, it is interesting to take a look at the way various segments of the media and the public deal with striptease.

Reporters and journalists will often not admit overtly that they are antagonistic to women's sexuality. Yet it is clear that the subject of strippers unsettles them. Look at this list of headlines taken from newspaper stories about strippers.

You can stop shaking
Strip shakedown
O-o-o-ps! Not in Kamloops, toots!
Nude beauty threatens different kind of suit
Beverly Hills bar to bump 'n' grind to halt
Stripper's road paved with bumps and grinds
Stripping bit of a grind
Strippers inciting not just delighting
Glamour gone-gone from go-go in the buff
Nude show barely fails to take off

When it comes to strippers, some journalists just can't resist making corny puns or cute cracks. But the jocular tone is a flimsy disguise for an attitude that is patronizing, and even sneering.

When stripper Gwendolyn did a standup comedy on a bill of dancers and performance artists, the local reviewer described her as "an alumna of the university of bump and grind," and commented that it was unfair that the audience was not provided with "the appropriate scotch and sodas or at the very least the lady's telephone number." He said nothing about her performance, which was, in fact, a brave monologue about growing up a bad girl in a world hostile to female sexuality.

The refusal to take strippers seriously is a strategy for invalidating them, and one that has been effective, with the result that many people who have no first-hand knowledge of strippers view them as absurd sexual cartoons. What we fail to recognize is that by invalidating strippers we invalidate women's right to a sexual identity. This can only help to impoverish all of us, since it deprives women of their enjoyment of their own sexuality, and also means that men can't enjoy women's sexuality without guilt.

Some journalists don't hesitate to condemn strippers outright. There is no shortage of articles and essays that describe strippers as mixed-up girls who need help, women who aren't very bright and can't do anything else for a living, nymphomaniacs, junkies or pill freaks, prostitutes, and enemies of society. The general public has a tendency to believe and promote such views, and it is common for politicians and citizens, primed by such biases, to band together in an effort to get rid of strippers.

A story that appears frequently in the news in some variation tells of the enterprising tavern owner who has been making piles of money since bringing strippers into his establishment. His neighbours, however, are morally outraged and rally together to put a stop to the entertainment.

In 1982, council members for a Toronto suburb decided they wanted all thirteen strip joints in their area closed. They didn't have the legislative right to make a clean sweep of it, but they managed to get rid of the smaller clubs and increase restrictions on the larger ones. The mayor of the area is quoted as saying: "It's not a substantially moral way to make a buck."

When St. John's, Newfoundland got its first strip club in 1982, residents got up a petition against it, and politicians tried to close it down. Someone described it as a "total desecration of a nearby war memorial." This is overlooking the fact that soldiers are usually among the first to patronize strip clubs.

People are not asked to be rational in such situations. They are not asked to define their terms, quote their sources, tell about their experiences, or explain their fear and prejudice. Nor are they asked to be more tolerant or open minded. It goes without saying that sexual entertainment is corrupt.

The underlying rule, especially for women, is that you can't be sexual and also respectable. Sexuality and respectability are mutually exclusive by definition. The very function of the concept of respectability is to disapprove of the existence of sex. With this logic in place, it is impossible that a stripper could be respectable or that a respectable person could be sexual. That is why Queen Elizabeth has never stripped, or exhibited any overt signs of active sexuality. Rulers and politicians must be icons of respectability, which means they must project an image that is all but neutered. Any sign of having a sexual identity, and the fall from grace is swift and devastating.

Inevitable assumptions are made about the sexual habits of women who are strippers. "Oh come now, we all know what you dancers are like," was the retort of at least one man when turned down by a stripper. Dragu reports being propositioned by a doctor in Montreal while being examined for bronchitis, and by a chiropractor she went to for a dislocated rib. Both men made sexual advances after Dragu told them, in answer to routine questions, that she worked as a stripper. Like many of her kind, Dragu soon learned not to tell people what she did for a living. But sometimes that didn't work out too well either.

There was a time when Dragu used to eat breakfast at Barney's, a greasy spoon on Queen Street in Toronto. She was chummy with Barney – they used to talk about his eye operations and her work as an actress and performance artist. One morning as she was paying her bill, Barney asked her what she was working at just then. She was stripping at the Zanzibar, but she told him she was teaching dance classes to children. Barney nodded and smiled, and said: "Saw you in the paper this morning." Dragu looked over someone's shoulder at the morning paper and saw the full-colour photo of herself, and the article about her job as a stripper on Yonge Street.

Soon after that, Dragu went to visit her parents in Calgary. Her mother told her that her cousin Ida had handed out photocopies of the article to all the relatives (although her father and her grandmother had spoken out in her support). More recently, Dragu visited her whole family, including cousin Ida.

We had a big brunch at a local hotel, and I took pictures of everybody. I knew Ida was itching to ask me something, and finally she turned to me and said she had read somewhere that me and another woman were writing a book. She wanted to know what it was about. I knew she already knew, but I didn't want to talk about it, so I calmly turned to her, looked her straight in the eye, and said: "It's a book of art criticism."

Once a woman asserts her sexual identity, she essentially loses her reputation. Dragu claims that she could win the nobel prize and she'd still be known as a stripper. Over the years, there have been many reviews of her work as a performance artist and actress, and not one of them has failed to mention that she used to be a stripper. We find it difficult to forgive women their sexuality, and will consider it only if the accused is willing to admit to her error and openly repent.

A magazine article written in 1962 tells about a young woman of good family left penniless on the death of her father. Josephine loved to dance, but her physique was too ample for ballet. She decided to become a stripper. The article is all about how commendable Josephine is for facing her downfall with fortitude, and for continuing to despise and condemn her chosen profession throughout her career.

A more recent newspaper story along the same lines tells of a certain actress who posed nude for *Playboy* when she was younger. Speaking about this to a journalist, she explains that she was broke and had a baby to support and didn't really want to do it. This, it seems, is her absolution.

When stripper Bridget went on trial on a charge of nudity in 1979, the crown counsel made a big point of showing that she was a stripper by choice. He first asked her if her husband was employed at the time she was charged. She replied that he was, at which he commented: "You weren't compelled to work at the Colonial, were you?" Bridget answered that her husband, a musician, sometimes went without work for several months, and that it was helpful when they could both work. Crown counsel asked: "But you weren't there by any kind of contract of indenture or slavery were you?" Bridget replied that she wasn't forced to work there. Later in the cross examination, he said: "Nobody's pointing a gun to your head to work at the Colonial and take off your clothes, agreed?"

The thought process evident here brings to mind the witch trials of previous centuries. Those trials were likewise perpetrated in the name of morality, and promoted a similar ethic. All might be forgiven if the accused has acted against her will and judgement, and doesn't actually believe in the life she is living and the work she is doing. Society reserves its compassion, its forgiveness, and even its respect for those willing to live without integrity. So threatening is the prospect that a woman might embody an independent, active sexual identity, that we would rather our women were victims.

IV

Revelations

We live in a culture where any expression of sexuality outside of adult heterosexual mating is, in some sense, a problem. Homosexuality, prostitution, incest, adultery, stripping, pornography – most everyone would experience some relief if these things went away. Our sexual code of ethics is rigid and exclusive. Its foundation is the centuries-old belief that sex is wrong and dangerous, and must therefore be closely regulated.

This belief is a part of our sexual history and culture. We are so closely allied with it that it is all but invisible to us. We don't see it as a belief at all, but rather understand it to be truth and reality. "Look what the stripper is doing," we say. "That's disgusting." We fail to notice that it is nothing more than the belief itself that horrifies us as we project it onto various sexual activities.

Strippers and other sexual workers put themselves on the line, not because of their sexual choices per se, but because, in this society, sexual offenders of any kind are outcasts. Our contempt for strippers has the same basis as our contempt for rapists. We condemn those who break the sexual code – at whatever level.

There are particular rules against sexuality in women. Only a hundred years ago, sexual desire in women was actually considered to be an illness, for which doctors prescribed treatments such as hot douches and blood letting. Today, we continue to mistrust sexually expressive women.

The low status of stripping is implicit in our sexual code. Stripping can only live down to its reputation, and thus obligingly reinforce our belief that it is an unwholesome activity. As we point the finger, we seem to be unaware that we are lost in a game of moral tail-chasing. Our views construct the parameters within which sexual entertainment must exist.

One way out of this dilemma is to consider strippers in their role of conscientious objector. From a historical perspective, strippers can be seen as women who are in active revolt against the dictate that their sexuality is shameful. A stripper may or may not have developed a political ideology around her work, but every stripper is aware that she is defying the sexual code, and many strippers have an instinctive understanding of the social implications of doing just that.

Historically, the taboos around women's bodies and sexuality have helped to create and maintain the low status of women. The device of women's clothing is an example of how this works. It is not very difficult to imagine the repressive physical and psychological effects of wearing many of the garments designed for women in the 19th century. For example, there were poke bonnets, which eliminated peripheral vision; tightly-laced corsets, which enforced shallow breathing and were painful besides, and sometimes caused deformation and even death; boned bodices, which kept women upright; as many as fourteen layers of petticoats, which made for considerable bulk and weight; metal-cage crinolines; steel or wire bustles; drop shoulders, which restricted arm movements; tied-back skirts known as the single trouser, which made walking difficult and running impossible; and finally trailing trains and abundant drapings and flounces, which made it necessary to move about with extreme caution.

Women's clothing was designed to cover the body almost completely, and in many cases it created a formal, stylized body shape, which served to distort and thereby hide the body's natural contours. The fashions described were accepted, in their time, as decent and respectable dress for women. To rebel could only invite social ostracism. At the same time, such clothing literally dictated repression, for to live in perpetual physical discomfort makes it difficult to move, and almost impossible to think.

What is interesting here is that the rules for covering, disguising and inhibiting the body were based in the belief that women's bodies are shameful. In other words, the bias against women's sexuality has been a major device for keeping women out of the world. So many of the rules of conduct that apply only to women spring from this bias. Real equality for women can only come with the acceptance of women's sexuality, and the release of all taboos associated with it.

Sexual equality would mean a lot for women, but it would have vast implications for society as a whole. For example, prostitution would probably disappear, or if it did not disappear, then it would be shared as a profession by men and women alike. If female worth no longer rested on chastity, then women's bodies would not be in any greater demand than men's as sexual objects. Also, because there would be no particular stigma attached to women's sexual activities, the attitude of contempt towards women in sexual contexts would evaporate. The school of pornography that depicts the sexual abuse of women would no longer have any social basis or meaning.

If we did have sexual equality, then sex in general would probably enjoy much greater acceptance, since it is women who carry the sexual taint. People would be able to enjoy sex at more levels and in more contexts. If we did not repress our sexual feelings they would not become distorted by guilt, and perverse sexual attitudes would have no context in which to flourish. Sexual entertainment would evolve and improve, and would become more meaningful for both men and women. All of this is simply to say that sexual repression in general, and particularly the repression of women's sexuality, is at the base of our sexual distress as a society.

Women have gained a lot of sexual freedom over the past hundred years. Some of the credit for this must go to sexual entertainers, for it is impossible to make this kind of gain without women who are willing to work on the cutting edge of sexual change. This can be seen more clearly in a historical context.

For example, during the late 19th century, women's legs became a strong focus for moral outrage. It was a time when even the mention of women's legs was considered to be shocking and indecent. The word *limb*, and the French word *jambe* were used as euphemisms. Women's legs were of course completely covered and disguised by voluminous skirts that generally touched the ground. The so-called short skirt that came and went during the period never fell shorter than ankle length.

The general infamy associated with women's legs is brought home by the story of a gift of silk stockings that was offered to a Spanish queen on the occasion of her marriage. The stockings were refused with the rebuke: "The Queen of Spain has no legs."

In defiance of this trend, women entertainers in New York, Paris, and London began showing their legs in the theatre. The thing was to wear tights, and thus reveal the clearly delineated form of the leg without going so far as to actually expose the flesh. The most daring displays featured tights that were flesh-coloured to simulate nudity.

The uproar these shows caused can hardly be believed. An actress of the period said that every time she revealed her tights-clad leg through the slit in her skirt, it was greeted by great guffaws from some of the men present. Meanwhile, ministers, politicians, suffragettes, and other morally-minded people organized campaigns and demonstrations in attempts to stop the outbreak of so-called nudity and vice.

The battle continued for many decades, and then, towards the end of the century, women's fashions began to change. In 1895, bloomers worn with thick stockings became a popular cycling costume for women. The bloomers of the time were so voluminous that they served, like skirts, to disguise the form, but they ended just below the knee, and so revealed the shape of the calf and ankle. This costume scandalized a great many people, and some bloomer wearers even had stones thrown at them, but the more daring continued to wear them.

In the final decade of the 19th century, skirts began to narrow at the ankles, coming dangerously close to acknowledging the existence of the lower leg. It was soon after this that the slit skirt came into being. Here was a fashion that finally admitted the lower leg into society, for slit skirts were worn at fashionable gatherings and with transparent stockings. From here, it was an easy slide into the 1920s, when women were wearing their skirts to mid calf. It should be mentioned that it was only with this initial acknowledgement of women's legs that it became plausible for women to wear trousers.

The movement continued to its logical conclusion, culminating with the miniskirt of the 1960s, and the total acceptance of pants and shorts as street wear for women. The result is that women's legs have been completely destigmatized. As far as legs go, women have gained equality with men.

This one breakthrough, which took a hundred years to achieve, has revolutionized the lives of women. The physical advantages range from suntanning to free movement. On a professional level, the change has allowed women to make a place for themselves in sports and jobs that were formerly open only to men. The purely psychological benefits are unknowable, but undoubtedly great.

It is impossible to say how much the leg revolution was helped along by the women entertainers who began by showing their legs in the theatre. The First World War did a lot to bring in practical and comfortable clothing for women. But considering the hysteria that greeted the first exhibitions of women's legs in the 1860s, it was probably vital to do some initial work in the formal and relatively safe arena of the theatre.

Many Victorian sexual taboos appear ridiculous from our present perspective of relative emancipation. We can now laugh at things like bathing machines, which provided women (men did not use them) with curtained steps so that they could descend into the ocean without being seen, in the interests of modesty, even though they were absurdly overdressed for swimming by our standards. And yet, the way we think about sex today is essentially no different from the way the Victorians thought about sex. We are more liberal, but we are quite as self-righteous and single-minded when it comes to our sensitive areas.

Strippers and other sexual entertainers undertake the job of pushing on our sexual limits in one way or another – by testing them, defying them, or even just exposing them. Sexual entertainment in the theatre provides an interesting cultural exposition, and because it informs the leading edge of sexual propriety, one of the things it can show us is where we are heading in terms of our sexual evolution. With this in mind, it is very telling that female strippers are becoming a thing of the past in some of the larger, more permissive western cities such as Berlin and New York. The progressive trend is to trim sex shows down to exclusively physical values. This doesn't quite come off in the striptease context, and is evidently confusing and demoralizing for the few strippers that persist in the midst of these values. As an example, here is Dragu's description of her visit to a New York strip club.

The Melody Berlesk was in the 42nd Street zone. A sign outside proclaimed that "berlesk" still lived there. My friend and I walked up the stairs to an old-fashioned theatre, similar to Le Strip here in Toronto, with rows of seats, a runway stage, and no booze. It was about six bucks admission. Elevator muzak was playing as we took our seats. There were five other people in the audience – none of them sitting together.

A voice introduced the first stripper, and a girl left the dressing room and walked up the stairs to the stage. The first one was so forgettable I can't remember a thing about her. The second stripper was a black girl – quite elegant in old-fashioned stiletto heels and a few pieces of lilac chiffon and a g-string. She had a nice presence and strutted well. She quickly whipped off all her clothes, including her g-string, sat on a chair in the middle of the runway, and did a long spread show. She had good form – pointed her toes and was smooth as butter – but she was very distant and disinterested. After her act, which closed with a faint smattering of applause, there was more muzak and a five-minute wait.

The third stripper came out – an energetic, chunky blonde in a sparkly aquamarine costume of bra, panties and g-string, all matching and very off-the-rack. She actually danced to the muzak! She was in her mid thirties and had a pot belly. Her smile glittered like fake jewels, and her eyes were hard.

She took it all off lickety-split, including the g-string, laid down on the runway, and got down to some heavy tit rubbing and a split beaver presentation to the bald guy sitting front-row centre. She spent a good ten minutes on her back, wiggling around and moaning and laughing and rubbing and receiving a steady flow of one-dollar bills from the bald guy. He never smiled once – just continued to shell out the bills. She milked him and milked him, like a porno-puppet cash register.

At one point her music stopped dead mid song – some kind of technical problem. She just sat up on the stage letting her belly hang out and started to count her money. One of the guys a few rows over called out to her in the silence, asking if she was mad about the music stopping, and she answered, "Nah, as long as I'm getting tipped I don't give a fuck."

She sat like a greedy four-year-old with candy, mesmerized by her money and counting and recounting it until the music started again.

This time it was even more dreadful wallpaper-type muzak – show hits from old Broadway productions done in saccharine arrangements of a thousand and one strings from elevator land. Truly horrible. She wiggled down onto her back and finished milking the unsmiling old bald guy until the song was over, then collected the rest of her money and her clothes and split.

The most recent formal innovation in sex entertainment is the private booth, where patrons can watch coin-operated video on small screens; or look at live shows through peepholes that have coin-operated shutters. Some of the booths provide for a degree of contact with a sex performer in an adjacent booth. The private booth allows a patron to select a specific product, and to interact privately with that product. It also allows him to make a minimal commitment to the product, since each dollar buys only a few minutes. Thus, sex is neatly commodified for individual consumption.

Meanwhile, the content of sex shows is becoming more explicit on a purely physical basis. Pornographic video makes no attempt to introduce emotion, atmosphere, romance, intelligence, or any value other than that of physical explicitness. Currently popular are closeups of the sexual organs and juices of man, woman and beast; interminable views of sexual poking, rubbing, pumping and sucking; and sometimes representations of physical abuse. It is fascinating that we have come to a point where this is what we produce and consume as sexual entertainment, and in many ways it seems appropriate.

We have always focused our suppression of sex on its purely physical aspects, and so it is natural that we also pursue sexual revelation at the physical level. We have projected our desire (as well as our guilt) onto the physical body, particularly the female body, and have proceeded to strip it bare in order to interact with our desire. This a perfectly valid process, and one that has served us well for a long time, but we seem to be reaching the end of the line. At one time, a passing glimpse of a woman's ankle could make a man feel faint with excitement. Today, even a good long look at a woman's inner labia is losing its charge.

We have revealed that which was forbidden to be revealed, and made it accessible to almost anyone who wants it. The exposé is nearing completion, and the vital question is: where do we go from here? If we stay within our present system of values, all we can really do is to continue along the same lines, and since we have about covered the common ground, that means we must create representations of more novel, exclusive and fetishistic sexual acts.

In this way, we are making a gradual shift in focus, and this shift is a real turning point in our sexual culture. The form is outreaching its social function, which has so far been to challenge and expose the repressive rules of the existing sexual code. We are now beginning to make sexual entertainment that has no basis in our commonality, and therefore in most cases, no basis in our actual desire. We have come to believe that sexual thrills lie in the realm of the forbidden, so we must seek out whatever remains forbidden and go there.

Sexual entertainment may be moving into decadence, but there is no point in blaming it for our problems. The underlying issue is our massive sexual dissatisfaction as a culture. No matter how far we go into the sexually explicit or bizarre, still it is not enough. For a century, we strove to uncover the female body, and when this finally happened it did not bring fulfilment. We have not found the sexual entertainment that enables us to sit back and say: "This is good. This is satisfying." We have learned to equate fulfilment with novelty, and within that equation satisfaction is impossible.

In New York's modern sex emporiums, one senses a growing hysteria at our inability to make sexual representations that are deeply satisfying. The sexual entertainment available there is like fast food. We may crave it, and keep going back for more, and even exist on a steady diet of it, but it is not enough. We are complex beings, with many different kinds of needs. Sexuality is complex, and exists as an emotional, intellectual and spiritual need as well as a physical one.

We are caught in a moral loop that involves the alternating repression and expression of physical acts of sex. So focused are we on this fascinating dichotomy that we fail to see a universe out there.

V

Vice

On one team we have strippers, prostitutes, b-girls, club owners, some comedians, drag queens and pornographers. On the other are vice cops. The game is called V-I-C-E and the first object is to make a living. The second object is to have your way with the other side. And the third and highest object is to make your point.

In the vice game, each side is peculiarly blind to the fact that the other side has points to make. Strippers, for instance, rarely see themselves as a social or moral menace, and think the policemen who arrest them are jerks. Vice cops think of strippers as naughty children, always trying to get away with something. If the police relax their control, strippers will take more chances – "Like kids in school who do something bad the minute their teacher's back is turned," as one of them put it.

But, in fact, both sides have a strong evangelical bent. To Montreal's Commandant De Grâce, for instance, all strippers are also prostitutes, and prostitutes are class victims. Wipe out prostitution and you will save countless future generations of women from lives of misery.

Some strippers, on the other hand, are dedicated to liberating society from sexual guilt and paranoia. A stripper exists "on the cutting edge of social change," as a Vancouver journalist says, "and whether or not she has thought about it, she is to a very large extent making radical statements every time she gets up on stage and drops her pants."

Every country plays its game of vice by a different set of rules. In Canada, the big issue of the past decade has been the g-string. In Germany they would just laugh if you wanted to talk about g-strings. The concerns there are more along the lines of keeping animals off the stage. But wherever you are, you can be sure the rules are complex, change all the time and are open to endless shades of interpretation.

In Canada, laws are made on federal, provincial and municipal levels. As one vice cop said: "No matter how many laws there are people will find ways around them." And as I was thinking when he said it: everybody but everybody wants to get in on controlling people's behaviour.

The federal law most used to bust strippers is the one that prohibits nudity, which is defined as being dressed in a way that offends public decency. This is a law that weathers well. It can keep pace with the times and adapt to the standards of any community. It can be interpreted as necessary from province to province, from month to month and from cop to cop. Meanwhile, ongoing court battles over the definition of the term "public" and the question of whether or not it is offended really keep players on their toes. Never knowing for sure whether or not you're breaking the law is one of the most thrilling aspects of V-I-C-E.

City laws tend to be clearer. For instance, a Montreal bylaw forbids strippers to mingle with, drink with, dance with, or sit at the same table with a customer. And in Toronto, it was illegal until just recently (and probably will be again) for a stripper to remove her g-string.

On a provincial level we have the liquor boards, which everyone says are not supposed to legislate morals but do. In 1974 the Ontario liquor board put a stop to dirty-talking comedy team MacLean and MacLean by threatening to revoke the liquor licences of clubs that hired them. MacLean and MacLean were out of the game, at least in Ontario, for almost a year before the liquor board got its hand slapped by higher powers. Meanwhile the B.C. liquor board has managed to keep audience participation out of strip shows – no help with zippers, no tucking bills into g-strings, no contact at all.

Players on the nightclub team step sharply to the tune of a liquor board because it's game over if you lose your licence. Otherwise, anyone's approach to the game and its rules depends on his or her politics, experience, position and style.

V-I-C-E is an unusual game in that there is never a winning team – there are only coups. Personal coups and political coups happen all the time on both sides. But neither side will ever admit defeat. There is no end in sight.

Vice in Montreal

Nude dance ruling could explode on city
Cops and strippers play waiting game
Nude striptease ruled not obscene
En matier d'indecence, on march sur des oeufs
Pour faire peur a un patron de cabaret dites "3416"
Strip clubs still have cold feet

Fabulous, passionate and Catholic Montreal – nightclub glamour centre – hot, hot town – everyone says Montreal strippers are special. Perhaps it's because even the gilt-dripping, opulent churches look like strip theatres. History. Home of famous strippers like Rina Berti, the singing stripper who is still talked about in Miami Beach and farther. Lili St. Cyr once played at what is now a high profile live theatre on Ste. Catherine. The Monument Nationale, where the National Theatre School is, was also a strip club.

Stripping is firmly rooted in Quebec culture. When I worked there it was still common to be stripping in a variety-style nightclub on a bill with contortionists, fire-eaters, chanteurs, live bands. "Good evening ladies and gentlemen/Bonsoir tout le monde, ce soir chez Lodeo je vous veux presenter la belle Nicole!" Nicole dances to a semi-rock country and western band. She is sandwiched between Oscar the Magnificent, who sits on nails and extinguishes cigarettes on his tongue, and a four-hundred-pound mama who sings racy songs and tells racier jokes. As the scrap metal collector at Le Relais used to say, taverns have always been where you escape the church to discuss politics, drink beer, celebrate, be a community. At Le Relais, after my last set on a Friday, a sailor who has been there all week serenades me with his guitar while the audience cheers. East of Frontenac, a Popeye Motorcycle gang member sits front row centre, and after I remove one stocking, weeps openly. He shakes my hand after the performance. At the Shack, an agent comes to give the girls a red rose each for opening night.

Close to the sci-fi Place d'Armes metro station in the heart of old Montreal (old churches, strip clubs, the court house) is the police station where I talked with Commandant De Grâce of the morality bureau. Up an elevator, past frosted glass, careful security and secretaries is the Commandant's sparsely furnished office – green filing cabinets, a desk and not much else. He is tall, attractive, pushing fifty, balding, bright-eyed, moustached, dressed in a dashing and well-fitting three-piece, camel-coloured suit. The vest is tightly buttoned and his tie is snug. He is passionate and fiery, committed, Catholic and evangelical. He introduces me to his young sidekick – blue jeans, longer hair, a real go-getter, and more out-of-control fiery than the Commandant, who is experienced.

G-strings are not required in Quebec. The Commandant says that in 1979 over a hundred strippers were charged with nudity for removing their g-strings, but the attorney general did not sign the orders so it stopped there. But one or two strippers are arrested each month for committing an indecent act. That means she touches herself or performs a sexual act with a customer or another performer.

The sidekick says there are many low nightclubs called "les trous" – holes. He says there are only ten "good" clubs in the city. They have "cute" girls, 18 to 25 years old with nice bodies. He showed me a business card from a "good" club – it had a small colour picture of a bunny type in a centrefold pose, and I thought, so this is "good" – but older women with sagging breasts and pot bellies are not "good". I guess that means, to him, ugly is vulgar, older is vulgar, non stereotype is vulgar. Or maybe women who are not bunnies do obscene things to compete in the bunny marketplace.

Commandant De Grâce says strippers are just a special class of hookers. He believes that strippers hook if they get a chance. "If you show your intimate parts, you will not be fussy about who you have sexual relations with." He thought it funny that strippers think they're better than street hookers because they don't have to take just anybody. They choose two or three admirers a week who give them dinner, a good time, sex and "gifts" – usually a hundred dollars. Strippers get wired on all that money, says the Commandant, and eventually, when they are too old or too tired to strip, or don't want to travel anymore, they switch to prostitution.

In my experience, stripping and prostitution are two completely different jobs – with a very small percentage of double jobbing. I kept thinking that I was glad I never ran into Commandant De Grâce in a strip club. I wouldn't want to be assessed by someone who was operating behind such a huge wall of prejudice and assumption. I told him I thought they were different jobs, and even so, what was wrong with the oldest profession – wasn't it a victimless crime? The Commandant and his sidekick were outraged by this idea.

The Commandant: "As a feminist you must be joking. As a woman you must be able to see this. Who becomes a prostitute? Not you. Not your daughter. Not my daughter. Not the upper classes. Not the middle classes. But people from low class families who cannot fend for themselves. Those with no education, no money, no support. Immigrants – legal or otherwise. They are the victims. And always there must be fresh meat. The prostitute's sexual power and her economic power only last for a short time. Then she gives her customers a younger girl and becomes a madam. Always fresh meat."

The sidekick shows me a file book of arrests – pictures of hookers from the Main. "How old do you think she is? Forty? Forty-five? No! She is twenty! This one? Twenty-one! She is used up – totally! This one? Ha! This one is a man – he just dresses as a woman. Look! Look at this one! And her! And her! Look at the eyes! The eyes show everything!"

I sat in my chair and was silent. What could I say to this Elmer Gantry and his second in command? They had a point. Still, I believed that society's attitude to prostitution was the problem. Things could be better if it was acknowledged and accepted instead of driven under. But the Commandant is completely dedicated to stopping prostitution – not controlling – stopping. He is zealous. This conviction is what makes him get up every morning and go to work and continue the battle.

As he talked, I sat thinking how easily I might have met him under different circumstances. As a stripper. He would have believed me to be "the lowest of the low" – someone who must be stopped. But there I was in his office, talking to him as someone researching the stripping industry for a book. I didn't tell him about my stripping background. What would be the point? This man, with his eyes blazing, his teeth and fists clenched, and his well-trained, go-getting sidekick ready to assist, was a stern patriarch doing what he believed right – with all his heart. I liked him, I feared him, but I could never agree with him.

What is wrong with his thinking? He is blinded. I am thinking about the French prostitutes' strike in Lyons when the women took refuge in a church to publicize their grievances about working conditions and show that they, too, were citizens and mothers and workers. To be recognized. Recognize. It is a political word for many kinds of groups – PLO, Red China. How can you not recognize an elephant in your bathtub?

While Commandant De Grâce is calling prostitutes (which in his books evidently includes strippers) "the lowest of the low" and "the lowest class of society," in another part of Montreal, former stripper Fonda Peters is saying the same thing about vice cops. "Morality is the lowest plane of existence for any cop," are her words. She reports that as a stripper she was often harassed by police.

"The police would come into the club, just up to their ears with all kinds of prejudice against me, and yet would very casually lean against the tape machine, smoking their cigarettes and drinking their free beer and make lewd comments like: 'Oh that was a very interesting dance, Miss Peters. This is modern jazz? Very nice, eh? Well me and my friend here, we're gonna go for a ride. You wanna come with us?' "

An innocent bystander might, at this point, actually smile to himself and think, "Gee. It's nice to see the cops being so friendly to strippers. I guess all is well with the world after all." But as Dragu says, if you're going to pull a break and enter, you don't drive up in a Lincoln Continental wearing red leather pants with two guys playing saxophone and yell: "Let's break the door down and steal the stereo!" Decoded, the above proposition reads something like:

"Say there Miss Peters, call it modern jazz if you like, but we could drag you through the mud for what you just did up there on stage. If you'd like to come out to the car, however, and give us each a blow job, maybe we'll let it pass this time. You strippers are all whores anyway, so it's nothing to you, and it'll make us feel like real men to grind some helpless stripper under our heels. Think about it while we finish this beer the manager has purchased for us hoping to sweeten our tempers a little."

This is a typical skirmish in the game of vice. A cop can pull this kind of thing anytime because it's never really clear what is being defined as illegal on any given day. Strippers all over town might have been happily removing their g-strings for years and then one day the cops start making arrests for removing g-strings. Meanwhile, club owners insist that the g-string comes off regardless, on threat of firing. If you're supporting a husband and a couple of kids, or if you're an illegal immigrant, or even if you're just young and scared, the last thing you want is to lose your job, never mind get dragged through the courts and have to pay legal expenses and possibly lose your case and be fined and, if you're an illegal worker, be deported. It's easy for a cop to play on your fears and win.

"It's very difficult to say no to these guys," says Fonda, "and you gotta let them off easy because this is your job and you don't want to create all kinds of problems."

Fonda Peters was a good player, capable of calling a bluff and getting off the hook at the same time. She knew how to let the cops down graciously, avoiding a summons and not arousing animosity, which could mean trouble for the club.

Another good player on the stripper team was Eve, who was famous twenty years ago for her Lady Godiva act. The wrinkle she used was a motorcycle instead of a horse. A novelty act. She started pulling in fairly decent crowds at a club on St. Denis. The vice squad came to check it out one night and she was busted. The papers reported it and she got bigger crowds and got busted again – and got even bigger crowds. The owners were happy as they laughed all the way to the bank, but when the cops came in a third time she revved her motorcycle engine and drove right off the stage, through the kitchen, out into the back alley, and zoomed around the streets of Montreal completely naked. Vive les Montréalaises!

Vice in Vancouver

Nude dancing ruled obscene but club operator acquitted
Judge watches nude dancers
Show not obscene
Nudity trial adjourned as lawyer, judge clash
Living in dark ages says trial judge
Nude shows acceptable, court plea
4 clubs decide to take it all off
Strip clubs taking off as court okays nudity
Exotic dancer charged again

Vancouver is a healthy place. The air, mountains, rain forest. Alberta calls it "lotus land." The mountains cut it off and make it look towards California instead of Toronto or New York. And because it is on the Pacific Rim, it also looks towards Japan and China. In Vancouver, you don't long to go to Paris, but you do long to get to Osaka or the Philippines. Vancouverites know the meaning of exotic.

The police station is located close to Chinatown and No. Five Orange, one of my favourite strip clubs. It's light, airy and cheerful – much less formal than the station in Montreal. On the walls are pictures and posters of city festivals and events. Acting Inspector Roberts is in his forties. He has closely clipped, thick, grey hair. He's wearing a light blue short-sleeved shirt, a wide tie and grey pants. He is worldly, calm, mellow, friendly – like the city he serves.

They haven't used the laws available for busting strippers in so long that the Inspector has to peruse the law books to find them. He tries federal first. Big volumes on his desk and in his lap. Is it 169 or 159? Close. 170. Nude in a public place or being clad in a way to offend public decency. But women haven't been getting arrested for taking their g-strings off here for a number of years. Back in '72, he says, the Kopenhavn Club was prosecuted for having an obscene performance which was a straight nude show. But that was ten years ago and public opinion has changed a lot since then.

The Inspector is uncertain when a performance should be considered obscene. He tells a story about a stripper at No. Five Orange. "She ran her fingers between her legs and licked them and took off her g-string and slid it between her legs and went to ring it out as if

'I'm all excited.' and, uh," he laughs, "this is a little embarrassing – she was able to make her genitals pulsate somehow. But just in case you missed it, she kept pointing to herself."

The Inspector explains that it doesn't matter what he feels personally about a performance. Everything depends on community standards. He sees his job as trying to reflect public opinion, not as imposing his own opinions on anybody or enforcing laws that nobody cares about. He mentioned, by the way, that there are about 40,000 federal and provincial laws governing conduct in Canada.

I kept thinking, as I talked to him, that if I had to get busted, this is the kind of cop I would want to face. Was it because he worked in a port town? I have a pet theory that Halifax and Vancouver are our most worldly cities because they are ports and have been dealing with the outside world more than the so-called sophisticated cities – Montreal and Toronto. The Inspector made sense. He even reminded me of a strip club manager I used to work for in Montreal – except Charlie smoked Export A and Inspector Roberts smoked extra lights.

I wanted to know if he thought strippers were all prostitutes – like Commandant De Grâce. He said very adamantly that not very many strippers work as prostitutes. Then he added: "Somebody – now don't take this personally – one of the members of our squad said that most strippers are dykes. And this may be, I don't know."

When he said that, I thought to myself: that member of the vice squad probably couldn't get a stripper to come across and decided to comfort himself with the old myth that they're all dykes.

Inspector Roberts took me down to the foyer. All the secretaries and other cops really liked him. We had a warm goodbye. I went out into Chinatown and hoped that his broad-mindedness filtered through the whole vice squad.

Vice in Miami Beach

State raids five strip joints here
Striptease ban goes on and off like on stage
Commission majority favours strip ban
Police close down all strip clubs on Miami Beach
Beach police shut all strip joints

I've always thought of Miami Beach as the east coast Las Vegas. It was the strip home of Honey Bruce – Lenny's famous wife. Big hotels, girls from France, gangsters, Jackie Gleason. And they do carry on the grand tradition of showbiz. I have never seen so much chiffon, burlesque top-banana humour, yadayadayada and sheer vaudeville. The average age of the populace is 86 with the strippers cruising at half that at 43. Tee Tee Red, a contortionist from Vegas whose kids learned early not to tell school friends their mama was a stripper has an act at Place Pigalle in which she winds two legs behind her head and rocks on her hands while telling jokes with punch lines that are banged up by a drummer who knows it by rote. He is so cool.

It was hard connecting with the vice team in Miami Beach. I thought I would never meet the famous Charlie. I had heard lots about him from a group of journalists and photographers who had "spent the night" with Charlie to cover stories, and they made him sound like a wild and crazy guy. He didn't work out of his office – he worked out of his car. Long, long hours at a stretch. I got the feeling he didn't really want to talk with me, but the department had okayed it and he kind of had to. Finally he arranged to pick me up at eleven at night. He came to my door and took me down to the car to meet his sidekick, Sluggo.

Charlie and Sluggo were real good old boys. Charlie was very country and western – white hair, slender, C&W shirt with the snap buttons, glasses, Willie Nelson kind of sexy, a face that had been around. He often used the cover of being a guitar player for the Kenny Rogers Band – I think he has a real fantasy about being a country and western star. Loves music. He had been president of the Optimist Club and got the lead singer from Place Pigalle to sing at a money raiser. It's a very small town – everybody knows everybody and it's all very chummy.

Sluggo was younger. Curly-haired, heavier. Charlie kidded him a lot about being college-educated. He had several degrees.

We cruised around the beach territory checking in with patrol cars and saying hello. No one quite knew if I was a hooker, a girl-friend, or what. The evening was young for them and they didn't know what to do with the Canadian Girl. We went to a big hotel coffee shop where there was a waitress Charlie had been getting coffee from for fifteen years – they were almost married – lots of real estate and general economy chitchat.

Finally Charlie tells me a certain hotel has been complaining about hookers in the cocktail bar and they're going to check it out. I can come along as an observer. If I hang out till the work is done – maybe two or three a.m. – they'll introduce me to everyone at Place Pigalle and that'll be fun. Will I be a sport? I say okay, as long as I'm not doing anything but observing. As long as I'm not contributing to anyone's arrest.

So we take off for the hotel. Charlie and Sluggo enjoy the hunt. We bomb around, them giving me a tough time – walkie talkies and guns in the glove compartment – a game of reaching over and under my leg to get the gun – good natured, ribald laughs. They're just like kids.

They're worried that it's my first time in a bar alone, especially the kind where people are looking to get picked up. They give me twenty dollars to cover drinks. We check into a hotel room and they set it up to look like two guys are staying there. Then they reverse the eyepiece on the door so you can see into the room from the outside.

We go downstairs and split up in the lobby. The detail is that if one of them is propositioned by a hooker, he takes her back to the room and, at a very discreet distance, the other one follows and listens and watches at the door. When he hears her offer her services for money, he walks in and makes the arrest. Lucky me gets to watch the whole thing, if I keep my eyes peeled and follow the action and tag along with the right guy. I feel like yelling: "The cops are here, the cops are here," but don't because it seems if I wasn't here, whoever is busted would get busted anyhow.

Sluggo loses out on a beautiful young hooker with a very expensive watch. She feels skittish, and when they get to the room she just won't say it and won't do it and suddenly jumps for the door. Me and Charlie have to hide on the fire escape so we won't be caught peeping. This is when Charlie really starts to loosen up with me. We giggle like school kids, but the edge is that we aren't kids. Charlie is an honest-to-god cop who is going to arrest people.

We go downstairs and start the whole process over again. More drinking. I'm on my third scotch. Lord knows how much Charlie and Sluggo have consumed. The city isn't paying for my drinks after all because this is a mingles joint and older men are hitting on me.

First a resort owner from New England who has buck teeth and greasy black hair and disco dances with me without looking at me, and then asks me in a businesslike manner about the possibilities of our "getting together tonight." And a bleary, blue-eyed ex priest turned piano player from New York who keeps patting my knee. All the while, Charlie and Sluggo are cruising by – separately – circling – and the bartender beams at me like an oily cheshire cat.

Charlie has scored two ladies, Sluggo says. I missed the pick up, but we are in the foyer, then the elevator. Sluggo is starting to sweat. "Odd business this," he says. Now we're outside the room. He whispers: "You feel like a voyeur sometimes." He is moving into the giggle state. The alcohol. The absurdity. He loves this game.

Through the peephole we see two 45-year-old hookers wrapped in towels. Charlie is saying: "Tell me what we'll do. I worry I'll get a heart attack." Suddenly I know this is it. She's going to say the words that will get them arrested. Real panic sweeps over me. Now Sluggo is in the room and I'm left in the hallway feeling terrified.

A while later, maybe ten minutes later, the door opens and they're getting ready for the move downstairs to the hotel security office. Charlie and Sluggo are like cats with birds in their mouths. One hooker, who looks like someone's mom, keeps saying, "I can't believe this. I just can't believe this." She's embarrassed. The other one just wants to know what's going to happen. And me – I can't understand why the taxpayers are paying these guys to rent hotel rooms and buy liquor and chase around these harmless ladies. It was Charlie who took them to the hotel room. It seems all wrong. Charlie and Sluggo are gloating. They stand back and whisper to me about this and that. Real proud. Really strutting their stuff.

Charlie says: "Ladies, we don't want to embarrass anyone. We're going to go down through the hotel to the security desk like old friends." Of course everyone in the hotel knows Charlie, and when the five of us go through the hotel there are waves of chitchat and laughter. Someone thinks Charlie has scored three hookers. Charlie yells back laughing, "Oh no, two is all I can handle. This lady is a writer from Canada."

We meet a big black cop in the security office. Lots of cop shop talk and telephone calls. Lots of polaroid camera shots for hotel records and waiting for the paddy wagon and tears and cigarettes and coffee and talk about one of the lady's asthma pills, and more tears and trips to the bathroom. I make coffee in the office coffee maker and hang out with the black cop who occasionally trades racist jokes with Charlie. We're all smoking a lot by this point and I can't drink any more coffee and I'm exhausted, and finally a young red-headed cop comes to put the ladies in the paddy wagon. He slams the handcuffs on this one lady and she asks, "Is this really necessary?" and he says oh yes, and enjoys it too much for my liking. He assures the other lady that a pair is waiting for her in the wagon.

They're gone, and I still can't figure out what they did wrong. But Charlie and Sluggo look smug. We get into their car. They admit that some nights nothing happens or you have to finish early if you're drinking too much. I start feeling nervous riding around with these drunk cops and their walkie talkies and guns, lost in a John Wayne movie. What am I doing sitting between these two guys? Real proud of me for not spending the city's money. Sluggo says: "Yeah, I saw a lot of guys really hitting on you." Laugh, laugh.

Because I've been such a good sport, it's time to go to Place Pigalle. They introduce me to Tee Tee Red and the singer M.C. and we have another drink. Everybody loves Charlie, even though he busted Tee Tee Red about six or eight years ago. Despite that, they have a certain camaraderie, Tee Tee and Charlie. We watch a large-breasted, chiffon-draped strutter who massages her breasts a lot and stops to talk real slow to a guy in the audience.

"I just can't respect that," Charlie keeps saying. "Strippers. Especially like that." Pointing at the Chiffon Queen wading through her set. Now Tee Tee is different. He doesn't respect her, oh no, but at least she's a contortionist and he can say that she can do something he can't do.

Finally Charlie just has to know why I would choose this subject to write about. Why stripping? Why do I want to hang around Place Pigalle and dumps like it? I'm a little high by this time and the evening is over, so I figure, why not tell him the truth. So I say: "Well, I used to be a stripper. I did it for almost eight years. So I'm interested in finding out what's behind it all, and what part it plays in society, and if it's the same everywhere or not."

Charlie and Sluggo are quite high too, but when they hear this, they sober up fast. It gets real quiet. For an instant, they look like they think I've pulled a fast one, like I've been laughing at them behind their backs. They look scared and shocked. They've been so busy treating me like the Virgin Mary, it hasn't occurred to them that I might be a stripper. They feel fooled – used.

We go out onto the streets, which are deserted except for a beautiful young Cuban couple kissing in a doorway. Charlie and Sluggo let out a blast of foul language in reference to the young woman. They call her douchebag, scuzzbucket, scum kinds of names, and add that she'll probably finish off her male friend right on the beach. They hadn't talked dirty at all before I told them my "real" identity.

We get into the car. This new attitude of theirs is giving the find-the-gun-and-walkie-talkie-kneesies game an edge that's not quite playful. I decide it's time to go home.

We pull up in front of my place and Charlie insists on walking me right to my door. The department is responsible for my safety. Wouldn't look good if I got knifed when out with the cops, would it? Upstairs, we pause and look at each other. I really don't want Charlie to feel "taken". I genuinely like him, despite the huge value gulf between us. What an adversary. I wouldn't want to get busted by him. For anything, even jaywalking. Yet he's been real straight with me and I don't want him to feel bad. I kiss him on the cheek and he smiles. And he's down the stairs and off for breakfast with Sluggo. I fall asleep nose down on my bed and wake up sad.

The next day I saw one of the photographers for the Miami News *in a restaurant. I knew this guy had ridden around with Charlie to cover stories for the paper. "Charlie's quite a guy, don't you think"? he asked smiling and looking at me knowingly. I said yeah, but wondered what his times with Charlie were like. I couldn't believe they had been anything like mine.*

VI

THE WORLD FAMOUS . . .
CRAZY HORSE SALOON
PRESENTS THE ORIGINAL
ALL NUDE MALE REVUE
EVERY NITE IS LADIES NIGHT
ALL NUDE MALE REVUE
SHOWS NITELY:
8 p.m. — 10 p.m.
Midnite — 2 a.m.
Open 7 nites a week
Reservations Available For all shows 949-3012
Men admitted only when accompanied by a lady
Proof of age required
CRAZY HORSE SALOON
16410 BISCAYNE BLVD. • NMB • 949-0565

The Cock's Dance

Male strippers talk about the screaming desire and thunderous applause of crowds of women, and about being drunk with the power of seduction. They earn higher wages than female strippers. Club managers, who are almost always men, respect them for their high earnings and their success with women. Their image is positive, upbeat and charged with good will. Journalists smile upon them indulgently, touting them as a system for female bonding, a replacement for church, an absolutely safe and guilt-free experience, a way for married women to get out of the house, laughs and a good time for wholesome girls out on the town, cute, crazy and fun.

This view stands in contrast to the popular view of women strippers, who are perceived as immoral, disgusting, disgraceful, sleazy, contemptible, bored, boring and out of date.

A scene in the movie "Flashdance" shows the female stripper's girlfriend marching into the club and dragging the nude and protesting stripper into the street to save her from a life of degradation. The scene takes a typical pop culture view of the female stripper, and one that would never work with a male stripper, or only if he were being rescued from a life of irresponsible fun and womanizing for a more serious pursuit.

No one is dragging men off the strip stage and no organization of men is accusing male strippers of degrading their sex. Whatever is unsavoury about women's sexuality and its display simply does not apply to men.

Yet the advent of the male stripper is a sign that sex is, in fact, becoming a more acceptable pursuit for women, who have worked to increase their professional status but have not, until now, thought to participate in sexual activities as men's equals. Victorian women were thinking about the vote – not the lack of erotic literature and imagery for women. More recently, women have been concerned with equal pay and opportunity in business. But until the last decade, stripping and other forms of erotic entertainment have existed for men alone. One of the remaining claims to be consolidated by women is the right to indulge their sexuality without loss of status. And while it is still seen as degrading for women to exhibit sexuality, sexual consumption by women is gaining acceptance.

It was at Montreal's Club 281 that I first witnessed a large group of women tasting the delights of sexual purchase. The club employed about two dozen male strippers, who waited on tables in scanty costumes when they were not on stage. All of the male strippers were also available for table dancing. For five dollars you could have any one of them come to your table toting a black box which he would put down next to your chair and stand on, so that his genitals were about eye level. He would gaze down into your eyes and strip to one song, removing all of his clothes including g-string.

At all times, there were at least half a dozen naked men in the club – one on stage and others standing on boxes undulating above the sea of appreciative women. Muscle and flesh were abundantly present and openly desired. It was a feast of the male body, without precedent, and a thriving enterprise based on men serving sex to women.

Male strippers have existed for long enough to be recognized as more than a fad. They are popular throughout North America, and supply a thriving marketplace of female consumers. Their existence reveals a break with the long, one-sided tradition of women as men's playthings – a tradition based in a notion of sexuality as a commodity possessed by women alone – the same tradition that creates the idea of the tainted woman and the corresponding dictate of sexual passivity as the proper mode for respectable females. The male, for his part, has been reared as a kind of sexual cavalier, required to vanquish this passive woman who lacks visible desire, and to make what use he can of the other kind of female. Given the situation, a man's clearest option is to channel his sexuality in terms of conquest and dominance, which is what has apparently happened to a segment of North American men.

In any case, the male sexual dance is an absolutely unprecedented phenomenon – a situation in which men assume the passive role of displaying body and sexuality in a narcissitic way as enticement to the opposite sex. This leaves women with the alternate function of admiration and pursuit, which they seem to enjoy very much. The male dance acts as a powerful invocation of the feminine libido, which is proving to be a force of some magnitude. The incredible energy and enthusiasm of women who patronize male strippers gives an impression of centuries of repressed lust finally becoming manifest in the rushing, flooding revelation of the female sexual drive.

Male stripper Jason Eros tells about stripping at a bridal shower in a Polish Hall. There were two hundred females in attendance, including a large number of teenage girls. After his show, more than a dozen of the teenagers stampeded his dressing room. They threw him against the wall and went straight for his groin, he says, grabbing and tearing at his clothes. (He somehow managed to escape before being injured.)

Adult women show better manners, yet in their way they are quite as aggressive. Jason tells about working at the Colonial Tavern in Toronto one night. He was performing with his cape – a large, voluminous garment which he sometimes used to enfold select women in a private embrace. One of the chosen, faced with Jason's jock strap at eye level as he stood over her, decided to indulge in the obvious temptation.

"She started giving me head," says Jason, sounding still amazed by her forthrightness. "And it was good head. Really good head! I just stood there till my knees got weak, and then I sat down on the chair beside her, the cape still wrapped around her head."

When he finally stood up again, his erection was obvious under his jock strap, which he had put back in place. The female audience screamed and cheered, and Jason proceeded to another likely-looking customer.

He reports getting head from three different women that night, and going home with two others who had passed him a note saying: "Do you want a threesome? Marlene and Marie."

I recall a woman at Club 281 who behaved with great aggression in a quiet, determined way. She had become fixated on one male stripper in particular, and bought repeated table dances from him. She bought him at least a dozen times during the few hours I was there. She didn't talk or smile, yet was obviously fascinated by both the stripper and by the power she possessed over him in the form of unlimited five-dollar bills. Such behaviour is a welcome inversion of traditional roles. The woman becomes the aggressor – the man the object of desire willing to capitalize on his erotic appeal.

It is true that male striptease is often styled on traditional male aggression. It can be the strutting and crowing dance of the cock, with the stripper flexing his muscles, doing handstands and backflips, posing and swaggering, and courting his female audience with charm and confidence. The most successful male table dancers know how to bend over and brush lips with a client, gazing at her with eyes that burn with desire, taking full charge of the courtship with the classic male technique of power and tenderness combined.

Of course, women strippers often do likewise, performing with energy, spirit, and confidence, and behaving in quite as forward a manner as their male counterparts. But the idea of sexual prowess in women is so foreign to us that we often fail to recognize it when we see it. Popular opinion is echoed in the statement of a columnist who writes that when women strip for men, the men are in control, and when men strip for women, the men are still in control. This is a matter of seeing what you believe, instead of the reverse.

But issues of power and control don't seem especially relevant to a discussion of stripping. Questions of power reduce to questions of status in this case. The idea of powerlessness on the part of the female stripper arises from a general disdain for the sexually overt female – an attitude that may be felt and reflected by a stripper, but is mainly a projection of the viewer himself. Likewise, any power accredited to the male stripper stands relative to this bias.

Without the prefabricated prejudice, stripping becomes an entertainment like any other, with one distinction – it involves the creation of a sexual commodity, or object of desire. The concept of the sex object is loaded with notions of oppression, but it is important to realize that unless there is something wrong with sex itself, there can be no evil in the creation of objects of sexual desire. The abusive attitudes that sometimes accompany desire are not inherent in desire itself and should not be allowed to taint our view of human lust.

Women – classically in the waiting, posturing, consenting position, haven't previously enjoyed a context in which they might feel and assert a sense of lust, and are now finding that their libidos are robust after all. The experience of sexual titillation outside of an emotional or romantic context is liberating for women. It is not that they are learning to suppress emotion, as so many men have been trained to do. To recognize sex as a discrete force is a refinement of understanding. Nor will active libidos necessarily lead women to a pornographic sensibility. Pornography always involves some form of abuse, and is a problem of attitude not arising from mere sexual representation.

At the male strip club in Montreal, I took particular notice of a young, beautiful and confident Indonesian woman who was sampling table dancers as though they were a new kind of fruit drink in eighteen flavours. One by one they arrived at her bidding and danced for her as she sat backwards on a bar stool, leaning her elbows on the bar and emitting rays of pure enjoyment.

I felt that my own pleasure in being there was as great as hers. I didn't indulge in table dancers as avidly as she did, trying only one, but I did feel that I understood at last why men go to strip clubs. I discovered that night that I could enjoy the sensual presentation of body and sexuality in a simple, organic way that had no relationship with anything outside of itself. It was, for me, the discovery of a new continent, and it seemed so concretely obvious once found, that I felt only incomprehension when the man who had come to the club with me, pondering the beautiful Indonesian woman enjoying her stream of hired dancers, wondered why she was buying her pleasure when she was so beautiful that she, as he put it, "could have any man she wanted."

VII

Honour and Jealousy

It's hard to know what came first – the strip club or the movie about it. Sometimes it seems everybody in the club is going around doing Bogart and Bacall – spewing tough-guy dialogue and bad-girl lingo like they were playing parts. The melodrama that goes down on a daily basis in clubs is often so predictable it seems rehearsed. The same characters enact the same scenes time after time, with only the details changing.

Dragu has participated in many such passion dramas, and has heard tell of many more. The stories cluster around issues of territory, status, lobbying for power and staying clean – important in every job, yet in the strip club it seems that peoples' true colours surface more often and more rapidly than in other places. The atmosphere draws people out – the music, alcohol, nude bodies and dim lights, as well as the traditional role of clubs as a place where people come to relax and let it all hang out. Dragu says:

Nothing Happened

A very sleazy and very popular scene at the club is called "Nothing Happened." This is a movie where everyone is staggering around trying to figure out what the plot is. If anyone wants to know anything, the right answer is:

"No, nothing. Nothing happened."

Just lie your heart out and keep on hustling, because all that competition, scrambling for money, and status-swinging creates a bed of gossip, lies, and innuendo in action.

Nothing happened in the office when I got my first raise. I was working the Frank-Sinatra-style Copa Cabana in Montreal. I was so young and dumb that I didn't know what to say when the owner took me into his office and offered me a raise.

"Gee – I don't know – what do you usually pay?" I stammered.

He said: "What do you want? Ten dollars more a night? Twenty? Fifty?" He was dying to do some dickering.

He finally gave me fifteen dollars more a night and made me promise not to tell the other girls what I was making. He didn't want them asking for more money. Divide and conquer was his policy – keep things secret and keep the girls competitive among themselves. That way they are less likely to gang up on you with some kind of organized demand.

"The second I hear anyone talking about how much Angie is getting," he said to me, "you are out on your ass!"

I was wide-eyed and thrilled with my raise as I left the office. Girls whispered to me as I went by: "Was it a raise? Did he give you a raise? What happened?"

"It was nothing," I told them. "Nothing happened. Nothing at all."

If there's one place on earth where nothing has ever happened, it's a room with a cop and a stripper locked inside. My stripper friend Bridget has been there when she suspected something was happening in that room, like the time two cops took a girl into the dressing room and locked the door. "It really looked suspicious," says Bridget. "Especially when the girl came out all red-faced afterwards."

But the girl claimed that nothing had happened in there. She said that her daughter had gone missing and the cops had some informa-

tion about her daughter. So even though these guys were just two plainclothes cops who had been sitting at the bar an hour earlier, the fact is, nothing happened in the dressing room.

Nothing happened in the alley either. On my first night as a stripper at the Zanzibar, one of the day girls stayed on to party into the night. She was a big, cherubic, fuzzy-haired lady with slightly glazed eyes. She brought her drink over and sat down with me and told me that she had gone into the alley behind the club with the boyfriend of one of the other dancers. "Just to smoke some hash," she said. Big catfight ensued. The other dancer was running around telling everybody about the fight, and that she had won. But the fuzzy-haired mama wanted me to know that the other dancer had her tits in a knot about nothing – because nothing happened in the alley. "We were just tokin' a spliff, ya know. Nothing happened."

Strange Allies

In movies where the stripper is cast as a not-so-shady character – someone who is actually human, with feelings and morals – then sometimes the movie will have scenes that are a little odd, but quite touching.

Gwendolyn tells about working at Cheaters two weeks before. It was her first day in the club and two businessmen came in. She noticed them because at that hour the clientele is mostly working class.

While Gwendolyn danced, one of the businessmen took out a camera. He snapped a picture just as she executed one of her skilful somersaults. Gwendolyn points out that she was in a compromising position and it was not the kind of picture she wants taken by a stranger.

"So I just stopped my show," she says. "I insisted on having the film. The bartender stopped my tape, and I told the audience, for fourteen dollars a show, I'm not having my picture taken."

The man with the camera asked, "Do you want a model's fee?"

Gwendolyn answered, "No, I just don't want my picture taken."

The other businessman asked, "Oh what difference does it make."

Gwendolyn replied, "You're sitting down there in a business suit, and I'm standing up here with nothing on but my g-string, and you're asking me what difference it makes?"

The other guys in the club – the working class faction – were all on her side. (Lucky Gwendolyn.) They all yelled: "Give her the film!"

The night manager had just come on duty. Gwendolyn hadn't met him yet – first day of work story. He said, "You do the show. Do the show."

Gwendolyn stood firm, telling him: "I'm not finishing my show until I have the film."

The night manager, lying, said, "I own this club. I am the owner," whereupon Gwendolyn replied, "And I am a dancer. Hello." Mexican standoff.

Everyone stopped and waited. Finally, the businessman took the film out of the camera and handed it over. "Then," says Gwendolyn, "we went on with the show."

Strippers and customers don't usually gang up together, but this was a working class coalition going in for a slightly odd variation of a workers vs management scene.

Here is a story of an even more strange and fleeting alliance.

Bridget usually does stags with a hooker because then her job is clearly defined. Bridget strips and goes home and the hooker stays and hooks. This one time was the only time she ever did a stag alone. She had booked the gig through another stripper, who said that the guys understood that Bridget wasn't a hooker and that she was just going to do her strip and that was all.

It was a big Italian wedding stag in a private residence. There were sixty or seventy Italian males, drinking. "I should have known better," says Bridget. "They showed 'Deep Throat' and then, when I went to do my show, they didn't want me to do a show at all. They didn't even want me to put my costume on. They didn't even have a tape machine. They wanted me to fuck the groom in the middle of the floor."

Bridget was not about to do this. She'd already got her money up front – a hundred dollars – so she went upstairs. She was going to get her bag and leave. It was getting nasty and she hoped she would be able to escape.

But the groom followed her upstairs and all the guys cheered. They thought that Bridget didn't want to do it in the middle of the floor, but she would go for it in the privacy of the bedroom.

In the bedroom, the groom offered Bridget thirty dollars to fuck him. She refused, explaining that she wasn't a hooker. She tried playing on his sympathies, saying, "You wouldn't want this to happen to your sister, or your mother, would you?" And she started to cry.

The groom felt sorry for her, but he didn't want to go downstairs and face his friends, who all thought he was getting laid. So he offered her thirty-five, then forty dollars to have sex.

"This is what's supposed to happen at stags," he complained. "I'm supposed to get fucked. Whether or not the other guys get it doesn't matter. I'm the groom. I'm getting married next week. I've gotta get laid."

Then he had an idea. "I'll tell you what. If I give you a hundred dollars, will you stay here for twenty minutes and pretend you fucked me?"

"That's Catholic economics," says Bridget. "To fuck him, he was really gonna haggle. He would probably have gone up to fifty dollars tops. But to pretend I fucked him, he would have given me two hundred."

Bridget agreed to the deal, but says that even though she didn't have to perform for the money, it was the toughest two-hundred dollars she ever made.

Politics makes strange bedfellows.

Cracking the Status Quo

Racism is a very big strip club movie. In North America, it is black women who are kicked downstairs. Orientals and Polynesians are considered exotic, but managers think their customers don't want to watch black women strip.

Denese wasn't allowed to work upstairs at the Colonial. It was fancier upstairs. Competitive. Lounge up and beer hall down. More paycheck money upstairs, though with tips you could sometimes take home more when you worked downstairs. But it was seedy and nobody liked working there.

Management was stupid not to do better business with Denese. They would tell her, when her hair was very Afro-short, that she looked too masculine. They asked her to do extras, like having sex with them or sitting with their friends. Denese says, "If you're not into it, they can't handle you cause then of course you're becoming superior. And there's nothing worse than a superior black, as far as they are concerned. I mean, let alone a superior lady."

Belinda worked upstairs. Not nearly as good a dancer as Denese, but lighter skinned.

Bridget says there was a period of time at the Colonial when Tina Turner could have walked in and offered her services for five hundred a week, and they would have turned her down.

Bridget told me about a black stripper who wanted to work at Gimlet's. "She looks like a Ugandan Princess – this girl is just incredible. She has amazing costumes and long beaded hair. She's about six feet tall. She kept going back to Gimlet's till the other girls began to pressure the manager to hire her. He was being pushed into the spotlight. Scared of a human rights scene if this got more public, he finally said to her, 'Well, you're not as dark as some of them.' "

Gwendolyn says she's not feminist, or Marxist, or anything. With her, it's "street politics" – just getting hip to how it all works and drawing your conclusions from that. For instance: "If there are five women in the bar and the heat comes in and someone is going to get busted, you know it's going to be the black girl."

Desirée is Toronto's favourite agent. All the girls love her. Desirée spent her youth as a travelling American stripper. She is very calm, with a soft, sweet voice. She solves all the girls' problems by phone.

Desirée has to deal with racism in the clubs. "Black girls gotta work too. How do you tell a girl I can't book you because you're black. Like, I am black. And it sounds kinda stupid saying I can't book you because you're black."

If a new client says to Desirée that he doesn't want any black girls, Desirée waits about two or three weeks, and then phones him up and says, "Look, I have this nice black girl and this is all I have. You can take her or you can leave her, but this is it." I haven't had one turn me down yet. Once I've got my girl in there, I have never had a problem getting another black girl in there."

She tells a story about a club in St. Catharines. This was about four years ago, says Desirée. "On Monday, I sent him a black girl. He called me up and said: 'You sent me a black girl and I told you not to. I'm going to be empty all week.' I said: 'I sent you a black girl and you won't be empty all week. You better not send her back, because if you send her back you're going in before the Human Rights Board.' So he kept her and had fantastic business all week. He asked her to come back, but the dancer said she would never go back there again."

I wish I could have seen Desirée dance – with the live bands and her wearing her Margaret Baker original striptease costume. "If you had a Margaret Baker creation, like you was really something."

Desirée knew about cracking the status quo. It isn't always easy, as Fonda Peters discovered. Fonda started Tits For Tots, an annual stripathon for charity in Montreal. Her idea was to raise money for charity while also making her statement that "We women are not just a bunch of empty-headed hussies." But nobody wanted her filthy money. It was hard getting an organization to say, "Yes, let's do it." There were rejections for a week until finally the Montreal Children's Hospital agreed.

The next step was finding a good club to do the show in. Fonda also needed the co-operation of the agencies to send girls. But it was uphill. Club owners wanted too much money at the door and were worried the benefit would scare away customers. Agents wanted to send the worst girls. Fonda got offers to split a cut of the money before it got to the hospital. Some strippers wouldn't consider doing a free show.

Every year there were new problems. The second year a French Canadian agent actually threatened to break Fonda's arms and legs if she carried on with the benefit. He was scared because it was starting to happen and the women were getting a sense of independence.

"Not that it changed anything, really," says Fonda, "but for one day the girls were high. They had the power. They were doing something and they were moving. You could feel it. And that intimidated the agencies."

Vets & Initiates

Being an actress, I've read dozens of movie scripts about strip clubs. When I was younger, directors had me read the part of the novice stripper who is just learning. When I got older, I started reading the part of the experienced stripper who passes on the tricks of the trade. Time marches on but movies stay the same. The scripts usually include a "mama told me not to come" rap, a heart-to-heart about age, men, sex and loneliness, a makeshift dance class or pygmalion-style metamorphosis in the dressing room, and a touching finale with the novice stripper "puttin' on her top hat" and wowing the audience. There is usually a standing ovation and sometimes a one-way ticket to Hollywood.

Meanwhile, back at the strip club, not too many strippers are making it to Hollywood, but there are always veteran strippers who are helping out fledglings.

Zaide was a modern dance student who stripped on Yonge Street in the early seventies. Her stripping debut is a classic. She got an audition at Le Strip by lying about her experience – she had none whatsoever. The manager had a closed-circuit video system. When he was in his office, he could monitor the dressing room, the front door and the stage. He watched Zaide's virgin flight.

The rules were that each stripper had fifteen minutes of music to do her act. The last five minutes of the show had to be done completely nude. At exactly fifteen minutes, the music stopped and the lights went out. The girls obeyed the rules because the manager fined them money if they broke any.

For her first strip, Zaide chose a costume that was a complete closet of clothes: stockings, garters, panties, bra, full slip, dress, jacket, hat, gloves, shoes – the works. She thought that since she was a professional dancer, stripping would be a snap. She got on stage and was dancing up a storm and having a wonderful time. Such a good time that she was zooming down to the five-minute mark and she still had most of her clothes on. Then she spied one of the strippers in the wings pointing wildly at her watch. This cued Zaide to madly rip off the rest of her clothes. But she was wearing so many that she barely got them off before the music ended and the lights went out.

The other strippers razzed Zaide a lot. They knew all about being elaborately but scantily dressed. Their costumes dripped rhinestones and sequins but everything snapped, zipped and velcroed off at the speed of light.

Later that night, the manager called Zaide into his office. He said, "You've never done this before, have you?"

"Oh, I have," answered Zaide. "I'm just really rusty."

He didn't believe her because he knew that everybody is lying in these movies. But he gave her the job anyway. She became a good stripper and changed roles from novice to veteran.

Bridget once took a naive young stripper home to stay with her and her husband. The novice, whose name was Kate, was twenty-three but looked like a highschool cheerleader and was as sweet and innocent as a baby, according to Bridget. She had come to Toronto from Calgary to go to York University. She stayed with her cousin till her cousin threw her out and then moved in with Bridget, who doted on her. "She followed me around like a little puppy dog," Bridget says. "It was nice, actually. And I took her under my wing because she was so naive."

Bridget was working at a Montreal-based, mafia-franchised club in Toronto. She was working doubles to save money for her clothing store. It was during the time when the g-string was a really hot issue in Toronto. Management was telling the girls to take their g-strings off and promising that they could protect them from cop problems because they were these Montreal mafia heavies. But Bridget had already been burned in a similar situation at the Colonial (the cops came in the front door and the managers ran out the back) so she opted to leave her g-string on, along with fledgling Kate and the other Toronto stripper.

Meanwhile, management had brought in three girls from Montreal. "To show us Toronto girls how it's done in Quebec," says Bridget. "This one girl was short and fat and she wore her glasses on stage. She danced in bare feet. She was a real pig. She used to jump onto the tables among the beer bottles and kneel down, without a g-string, and stick her ass in some guy's face. The guy put his head between her legs." Bridget found this disgusting. "Put an apple in her mouth and she would have been perfect."

Inevitably, the strippers split into two hostile factions. There were the Montreal strippers – the bosses' darlings, who didn't wear g-strings, and there were the Toronto girls, who did.

One day, in the thick of the rivalry, the pig stripper decided to pick on Bridget's fledgling. "Because Kate was so innocent," says Bridget. "I went into the dressing room one day and she had Kate by the neck up against the wall saying, 'You've been laughing at me and saying I'm sleazy. Well these guys tip me good and they think I'm really great and I'm just doing my job like you, so you better stop talking about me."

"So I hit her."

Bridget thought it was rotten of the pig stripper to pick on Kate when it was really Bridget and the other Toronto stripper who were doing the laughing. The pig stripper was surprised that Bridget hit her. Bridget was surprised too.

"I'm sure she didn't think I had it in me. I sure didn't think I had it in me. I had her up against the wall and I punched her. I think I got my knee in there too. Knee in her stomach. I was really mad. I thought she was going to hit me back, but she didn't. She could have creamed me."

Rivals

Rivalry between strippers can be a very big, ongoing scene at the club. Here is a story I call "Hamburger Toute Garnie." I can't tell what stripper this story happened to, or reveal what the basis of the rivalry was, but it was a long, heavy, escalating scene in Ottawa at Pandora's Box.

"Lola used to cut up my costumes, so I cut up her costumes," says Mlle. X. "Then she did something else and I did something back. It just went on and on, until this one day.

"She was a very beautiful lady, but she was a pig. There was an old man who used to give her money all the time, and she'd take his dentures out and rub them against her g-string."

X and another stripper were sitting up in the balcony one day watching Lola do her thing with the dentures. X and her friend both found it disgusting. They happened to be eating hamburgers up there. So X's friend suddenly chucks her hamburger off the balcony and gets Lola right on the side of the head.

"Can you dig this?" says X, gloating wildly. "This little Barbie Doll on stage with a hamburger running off the side of her face. Mustard, ketchup, the works."

There is a lot of territorial push and pull over the music strippers use.

Bridget comments that if a girl is breaking the ground rules laid down by the older girls in the dressing room, they just take her tape out of the machine while she's performing.

At the Colonial in Montreal, we used to dance to the jukebox, and I got into a fight when I used the same song as the most popular stripper there. The song was "Locomotion." The stripper's back arched and her nose went up and she told me that the song was hers. The manager had informed me that anybody could use any song on the jukebox. That may have been the rule, but I felt that for the sake of my health, it was better to back off. The stripper's whole personality seemed to be based on that one song. I remember a friend commenting that he thought she was dumb and not a great dancer, but "she had a bod that wouldn't stop."

Sequel: The locomotion stripper became a speed freak and her hair and skin started falling off. When I saw her again, she didn't care what song she danced to, you danced to, or if anybody was even looking at her. She was a vet – but she had switched movies to "Panic In Needle Park."

Bridget tells about dancing one night to a tape she'd never heard before. This was a tape the soundman had made for another stripper who didn't want it. The other stripper said: "That's disgusting, I'm not dancing to that." And Bridget said, "Oh, it's disgusting, I'll dance to it."

So she did. There were six songs on the tape and she did them cold. She'd never heard any of them before. It was dirty country and western stuff, and she did it as comedy, and it worked. She brought the house down. She felt as if the music had been made in heaven just for her.

After the show, the other girl, inflamed with jealousy, said to Bridget, "You're never dancing to that tape again," and she went into the sound booth and grabbed the tape.

Not to be beaten, Bridget had the soundman make a duplicate of the tape for her, and she's used it, but it never worked as well again. Bridget thinks it was the glorious sense of oneupmanship that made it all happen the first time.

VIII

TAVERN OWNER CHARGED WITH ASSAULT ON STRIPPER

Beaten with bat: Dancer

Girl-friend says she lied in Gargantua testimony

A witness at the preliminary hearing of Fernand Beaudet, charged with the deaths of 13 persons in the Gargantua Bar fire Jan. 21, testified yesterday ...

... 13 murders on his conscience.

The witness, now unemployed but a waitress at the time, swore yesterday these declarations were false and that she had made them to get out of custody.

She had been held, with several other persons, on a coroner's warrant pending the inquiry.

Ouellette, who was declared a hostile witness, was told by the judge: "I don't believe what you're saying today. You've been threatened and I understand ... but you're not doing much of a service to society... It's on your conscience."

Under cross-examination from

See TESTIMONY, Page A-2

'a lie'

Gunman kills 5 in North-End bar

... happened so fast," said Couillard.

"Some people said their backs were turned when the shooting started and they dove for the floor. . . . others say they were in the bathroom."

Brasserie d'Iberville shooting sequel

Trio guilty in killi...

PLUIE DE BALLES AU ROBERT BAR SALON

25 personnes ... par miracle

CRIME ORGANISÉ

L'ex-cabaret Chez Paree rouvert sous la... "surveillance" de la police

"MAD DOG" VACHON DOIT PAYER $5,400 ... SPECTATEUR DONT IL A FRACTURÉ LA MÂCHOIRE

HELL'S ANGELS GET RICH ON CRIME

News Services

NIAGARA FALLS, Ont. — Some members of the Hell's Angels in B.C. and Quebec have become millionaires through organized crime, a federal report says.

The report says motorcycle gangs across the country are a major organized crime threat whose members have become so sophisticated they conduct counter-intelligence on police.

The report was prepared by the Criminal Intelligence Service of Canada and was released at the annual conference of the Canadian Association of Police Chiefs.

It says the clubs have begun incorporating to avoid taxes and individual prosecution, and "some clubs are insuring the lives of their members and then sacrificing them later to collect the money."

It cites a recent case in Calgary, "where a club received $50,000 when one of its members was blown up in a vehicle."

The report says motorcycle gangs are heavily involved in the drug trade and murders related to that trade.

In some cities across Canada, police found that motorcycle clubs control the entire prostitution trade and placement of strippers in bars, it says.

The Stripper and the Gangster

Pluie de balles au Robert Bar Salon
L'ex-propriétaire du Robert Bar Salon perd $100,000 avec le clan des Dubois
Gunman kills 5 in North-End bar
L'incendie du Blue Bird avait fait 37 victimes

Nightclubs attract gangsters because they make ideal operating bases for all kinds of illegal activities, for example, drug peddling, pimping, gambling and the sale of unmarked liquor and watered-down drinks. The heavy cash flow and general commotion in nightclubs make good camouflage for illegal money and traffic.

Not all nightclubs are run by underworld types. "Just because we earn our living showing naked women, that doesn't mean we're gangsters," says a club owner in an Inspector Maigret novel. But a study of mafia news reveals that nightclubs are favoured bases for every kind of dirty business. Perhaps the most grotesque story I have come across is the murder that took place in 1975 at the Montreal nightclub called Chez Gargantua. Mobsters herded thirteen people into a closet and jammed the door shut with a jukebox, then set the club on fire. One of the victims was a topless dancer. Another was a taxi driver whose cab was found idling outside.

Because strippers work in nightclubs, it seems they must associate with gangsters. Certainly movies and detective stories would have it that way. As Raymond Chandler says: "These nightclub girls are apt to have some nasty friends." There are obviously opportunities for strippers and gangsters to rub shoulders, make friends, and become involved. But it doesn't bear out. Like the rest of us, strippers are on the outside, never knowing anything for sure.

Dragu, who worked as a stripper for several years in mob-run Montreal, still thinks of gangsters as men in fedoras who drive cadillacs and wear diamond rings on their baby fingers. This is not quite as naive as it seems, since gangsters do sometimes emulate their media image. In the tv documentary "Connections," which offered proof that an extensive, well-connected mafia network exists in North America, there was a shot of a known gangster walking in Toronto's Italian district. He was wearing a white suit, fedora and dark glasses, looking like he had just walked off a Hollywood set.

All the same, Dragu's idea of gangsters is not based on personal experience, and other strippers appear to be quite as poorly informed. Strippers bear witness to only fragments of mafia activity – obscure warnings, isolated bullet holes, mysterious ruins, rumoured threats. Stories of actual shootings come second and third hand. Every now and then a stripper dies, but for no better reason than being in the wrong place at the wrong time. The gangster stories that strippers tell make an odd collection. They are like ghost stories – producing evidence of gangsters, but never gangsters themselves. Dragu reports.

My first brush with the underworld happened when I had been stripping for about a year. I had a new agent who sent me to a club in Chateauguay – a racy suburb of Montreal. In Chateauguay we took our g-strings off.

I was working with old-timer Iris Rose – a transsexual stripper who had been around. Iris was tall and graceful with flowing blonde hair. She was the star and I was second banana. She was to report on my performance to the agent.

Iris taught me a lot during that gig and others that followed: not to lend or borrow a g-string – germs, to do an extra-terrific show if you were late for work, and if you were making big money to tip everyone on your last day and buy the manager a drink. Iris was a fountain of advice. She suggested that I wear red and black, that I grow my hair long because it would make my waist look smaller, and that I base my act on stockings and garters since my legs were my only good feature. I was overwhelmed by Iris' knowledge and experience. I followed all of her advice.

There was no dressing room in the club, so Iris and I took over the manager's office. We even kept an iron and ironing board in there. One night I went in to change and found the manager talking to another man. It was unheard of for the manager to be in his office at showtime. I didn't know what to do. I didn't want to change in front of them – I had made it a rule not to take my clothes off for managers and agents. To do that, in my books, was to lose respect. But I had to get ready for my show. So I ironed my costume and waited around.

The two men were talking up a storm in French. Really animated. I couldn't understand a word because they were talking so fast. Finally, after five or ten minutes, the manager said to me in English: "Angie, you are such a sweet girl. So shy. Most girls in this business will undress in front of anyone."

I thought it odd that he spoke to me in English, because we had so far talked in a mixture of English and French. Soon after that the visitor left, remarking to me as I went that it was "nice to see a girl so shy in this business."

I changed my clothes and did my act and then joined Iris Rose at a table. Iris explained that the manager owed money to his visitor who was a member of "The Family."

"Oh girl," she said to me. "You better pretend to know even less French than you do. Because you might have overheard something in there that you should never have heard."

The manager's visitor didn't look like a gangster. He had dark greasy hair and wore a black vinyl carcoat. I hadn't noticed a diamond ring on his baby finger. But I spoke English for the rest of the week.

A couple of years later, I was back working at the Copa Cabana, which had been my first home when I was a novice stripper. This time it was during the frères Dubois scare of the mid seventies. Every day the newspapers printed another story about this French family of ten brothers who had broken into organized crime in

Montreal – previously the domain of the well-established Italian mafia. The Dubois were linked with the Calcé Theatrical Agency, which booked the strippers for many of Montreal's clubs. There were insinuations that the brothers were running drug rings and extortion rackets and dealing in child prostitution. Montreal was the scene of an ongoing war between the noisy and theatrical French upstarts and the silent and more sophisticated Italian mafia.

My girlfriend Eva, a former stripper, brought her boyfriend Mario to the club one day to watch my show. Mario was a well-known pop singer who seemed to know all about the gang goings-on in Montreal. After my set I went to talk to them and found Mario in a quiet Italian rage.

"Get out of here, Dragu. I don't want to have to come and get you before something heavy goes down – like I had to do for Eva's girlfriend Jane."

Mario thought it was dangerous to be a stripper in Montreal during those days of hot gang warfare. He said I was playing with a time bomb.

I ignored his advice but decided I was tired of working at the Copa. I telephoned a club I had worked at and liked, and got Mr. Earl. He sounded sexy and black. He told me to come over for an audition at eleven that night. I had enough time to do it between sets at the Copa. The girls at the Copa told me that Mr. Earl was black mafia.

I knew that the club had changed hands since I'd worked there. I remembered a hot discotheque in the front bar, and a swank, French cabaret-style strip club in the back.

Even after all the mafia talk at the time I found it hard to believe what I found when I got to the club. The disco was closed. All the liquor was locked away and the till was shut. The lights were out. I walked into the back room and found a topless woman bartender drinking scotch. There was also a hostess in an evening dress, and a skinny doorman, both wandering around through the piles of rubble and broken glass. I asked for Mr. Earl. The hostess said she remembered me. I remembered her too. She told me that watching me dance the last time I had worked there had reminded her of her own days as a stripper, and that she missed them. I took that as a compliment.

I climbed the stairs to the third floor. The manager's office was near the dressing rooms, where Eva and I have discovered a bullet hole in the wall after hearing that a couple of Pittsburgh gangsters had met their demise at the club. Those dressing rooms were where Eva had told me about going to our mutual agent Don D'Amico's funeral and finding that only two strippers besides her had bothered to show up. It was sad. Around the time of D'Amico's funeral and the Pittsburgh guys getting shot, Eva did a strip to Lou Reed's "Goodnight Ladies," and she added pistol shots to her tape. She began her act peering through the curtains that looked out into Ste. Catherine street below. Her dance was a tribute to all the strippers working during those hot times.

I had never worked for a black manager, and it turned out that I never would. I knocked on the office door. Muffled voices.

"Who is it?"

"It's Angie. I telephoned."

"Oh yes – Angie."

Long pause.

"Now is not a good time. Come back later."

I said that I would. I waited a bit and listened, then went down the carpeted stairs past acres of velour wallpaper and through a fog of that permeating smell of Labatt's Cinquante. My first thought was that Mr. Earl was making it with a dancer up there. But then as I walked across the broken glass and through the shut down disco I thought – no – he's in trouble up there.

A similar thing happened to Toronto stripper Zaide. She had been working at a club on Yonge Street, and went in to collect her pay one day. A bouncer met her at the door and told her the club was closed. He let her look inside. The walls and ceiling had been sledge-hammered, the carpets were torn up, the furniture smashed and chairs driven into the walls by their metal legs. Zaide decided not to ask any questions and to forget about her paycheck.

I never had any experiences with gangsters in Toronto, and I always thought that there was more organized crime in Quebec than in Ontario. Crime seemed to be part of the culture and texture of Quebec. But some say there is more power and money in Toronto than in Montreal. I guess it is just quieter in Toronto. You need a licence to strip in Toronto. They take your social insurance number and have you fill out forms and pay you by cheque. In Montreal it was always cash paid directly to you by the manager.

After doing research at La presse *in Montreal, I began to think that perhaps the mafia is more evident in Quebec because gangsters are cultural heroes there. Miles of newspaper stories have reported the activities of the Dubois family. Political campaigns have been based on the problems of organized crime, and Mayor Drapeau promised to rid Montreal of it, which of course he couldn't do.*

News stories linked the Dubois brothers to the Robert Bar Salon, a club in St. Henri that I worked at on and off. I remember that every once in a while some well-dressed guy would come into the club and stand still and look around, real quiet, with an escort of two guys standing behind him. Then they would leave. I don't know what that was about. Roll call? Image boosting? I never checked their baby fingers for diamonds.

Another stripper, Leah, claimed to have had an affair with a gangster at the Robert. An Italian gangster, she said. Real mafia. Leah was very fussy about her men, and a romantic, but one night she decided that she wanted a particular gangster who hung around the club. She did a lot of bending over and looking between her legs and wiggling her bum during her act that night, letting him know it was him she was dancing for. She found it intensely erotic to make it with someone illegal and forbidden.

In January 1976 men in a passing car fired a rain of bullets at the Robert. I read about it in the papers. Perhaps it was this incident that Debbie was speaking about when I talked to her years later. Debbie was stripping at a sex circus joint on St. Catherine. We talked in the dressing room over rum and coke. She said she had been working at "Chez Robaille," or "Chez Rebaise" in St. Henri at the time when a big shooting happened. Did she mean the Robert Bar Salon? Or was she making it all up, perhaps remembering the story from the newspaper. She said the club was run by Dubois and that when the shooting started the strippers all hid in the dressing room downstairs. When they emerged after the scare they were all sent home with generous cash bonuses. The owners were real gentlemen, says Debbie.

During the hearings before a commission formed to investigate crime in Quebec, a woman called Denise, who was a former secretary of the Calcé Agency, testified that the Dubois were asking for 50% of the agency's profits. I wonder if this Denise is the same one mentioned by two of the strippers we interviewed. Stripper number one says that her agent in Quebec was Denise, who had given the agency's books to the police and was waiting for the mob to wipe her out, meanwhile drinking herself into oblivion. Stripper number two says that she had an agent called Denise – a woman who had set herself up independently and was therefore on the Dubois' hit list. Apparently Denise was sitting in a club one night watching one of her girls perform when a shot was fired. The bullet lodged in the upholstery of the booth Denise was sitting in. The club emptied of people immediately. The stripper was so scared that she ran outside in just her g-string and boa, and roamed the streets until she was picked up by police. A man who was with Denise ran into the kitchen and locked himself in a freezer. Many pairs of shoes were found under the tables after the incident.

This small collection of stories with no proper beginnings or endings is more folklore than fact, yet it does factually represent the kinds of associations that strippers have with gangsters. Strippers live in a world far removed from the inner circle of crime. Our research did not turn up even one stripper who qualifies as an insider.

The only story Dragu and I have heard that involves a first-hand encounter with verifiable hoods comes from a stripper who reports working at a Montreal club called Kojak Bar run by guys who had shaved their heads to emulate the TV cop. When they paid her at the end of the week, says the stripper, there was a gun on the table.

Dragu herself is not absolutely sure if she has ever known a gangster.

Men were always claiming to be gangsters back then. One short, middle-aged regular at the Copa said to me one night: "I am Daniel Dubois, the eleventh brother." He told me his wife was a former stripper who ran an agency. He suggested I grow my hair long and wear bangs because I would look cute that way.

I knew he wasn't really a mobster, but I was never certain about a man I met in another club. This man was charming, elegant and attractive. He wore expensive clothes and smelled good. He came to the club regularly in the afternoons, and he liked to talk about the country or politics or food and wine.

One day, he brought french bread and paté to share with me for lunch. After we ate, he told me he was a hit-man for the mafia. I didn't know whether to believe him or not.

IX

Boss Daddy

Dragu has a certain romantic reverence for paternal men. She is sentimental about managers and agents she has worked for over the years, and uses the same words of praise for all: fair, kind, good-hearted, avuncular, and charming.

She remembers her first agent, Angelo, as a kind and helpful man. He advised her to change her name from Margaret to Angie. His choice came from the Rolling Stones' song of that name, which Dragu frequently used as stripping music. Angelo also advised her to speak French as much as she could. "If anybody asks you if you speak French," he told her, "always say 'un peu,' and every day try to learn a little more." She could phone Angelo day or night, she says, with any little problem she was having at work, and he would always solve it for her.

There was her second agent, Don D'Amico, who always treated his girls with respect. He appeared at the club on their opening nights with a red rose for each of them.

There was Mike, a bouncer, who was smart, and could smell trouble before it materialized. One night when Dragu was dancing, a group of students in the audience started getting too loud and rowdy. Mike came on stage, swept Dragu up in his arms, and carried her (as you would carry a bride, she says) to the main stage in another part of the club. "You don't have to dance for those animals," he told her.

There was the agent who wanted to help Dragu save money to become a teacher. He had a plan. He would do advance promotion and publicity, and tour Dragu through the province of Quebec. In a year she would be able to save enough money for her entire education. He thought Dragu was too smart to be a stripper.

The Teddy Bear manager was rotund and kind. There were aerial swings in the club he ran, and when it was time for a stripper to go up on one of the swings, if he noticed she was on drink or drugs, he put someone else in her place. Dragu says:

You would do anything for this guy, he was like your dad. I came in really stoned once on heavy hashish. I changed my clothes and sat down in the dressing room and melted into the mirror. I was so wiped. And he came in and took a look at me and said: "I'll let you come down from whatever cloud you're flying on, and I'll be back in about 20 minutes. Do you think that's enough time?" And you knew that he didn't know anything about drugs. He had no idea what drug I'd taken – whether I'd smoked or popped a pill or whatever, but he had been around long enough to realize that the best way of dealing with these things was to be calm and roll with the punches.

There was the manager who collected Humphrey Bogart films – a small, elegant Frenchman in a pin-striped, three-piece suit who could stop a bar fight single-handed, and who once threw a guy out of the club for touching Dragu's ankle while she was dancing. "My hero," Dragu remarked to me, not joking. This same manager once gave a stripper friend of Dragu's a bathtub that had come out of the hotel upstairs from the club. Dragu found this very touching. And she was thrilled when he told her that as a performer she was both sexual and theatrical, and not only that, she was dependable.

It seems to be the combination of power with a caring and nurturing quality that Dragu finds compelling. Club managers in particular tend to embody this pair of traits. Managers are boss-daddy, father-protector, patriarch-lover. Dragu sees them as smart, attractive, experienced and wise. They know how to keep everything running smoothly, in spite of endless headaches with customers and employees. Dragu says:

They call you "little girl." They are proud to show you off. It's a good feeling to have someone proud of you. (My daddy sat me in his lap and sat back and looked at his little girl proudly. We were blood close.) Managers sit back and look at you proudly. You make them money. The more money you make, the prouder they are.

The need for approval from a male authority figure can get women into serious binds. This became graphic for me when Dragu told me about Cindy and Nick, a stripper and manager at the Toronto club where Dragu made a brief comeback as a stripper in 1982. "If Abraham was the first patriarch," says Dragu, "Nick was the second."

Nick hated blacks and greasers, didn't believe in contracts, and thought all strippers were whores. Nick's wife worked in the kitchen of his club and he treated her like dirt. "A family place," Dragu observes.

Cindy was slender, lovely and flawless. She lived in a suburban condominium with her mother and brother, who often came to the club to watch her show. She worked for Nick five days a week, and he completely dominated her. Cindy had been hired as a stripper, and was paid the same as the other strippers, but personal favours to Nick had become part of her job. He ordered her about in a rude and demanding way.

"Cindy! Phone! You deaf?"

"Cindy! Get me a coffee!"

"You work here?"

She did work there, and she jumped to obey him.

As a stripper, Cindy was skilled and energetic. Her specialty was floor shows. She did splits and backbends in a style that was intensely erotic. One day, soon after she came to work for Nick, she impulsively came down off the stage and got up on a customer's table to do her floor show. After that, Nick began to insist that she work the tables on a regular basis. He would sit down with customers while Cindy was on stage, and call her over in the middle of her dance.

"You work here?" Showing off to the customers. And Cindy came and did her backbends on the table among the glasses and beer bottles, her lovely, lean body stretching and pulsing just inches from Nick and his customers. Afterwards, in the dressing room, she cried with frustration.

"I hate it when he does that."

But she never complained to Nick, and she never refused him anything.

Dragu's relationship with Nick was clean. "I see all the hustles coming a mile away," she told me. "I avoid the squeeze. He never asks me to answer the telephone."

It wasn't always so with Dragu. In 1982, at the end of her stripping years, older and wiser, she could say such things, but her susceptibility to the patriarch was one of her most serious problems as a stripper.

Dragu's first unpleasant encounter with a manager was at Montreal's Copa Cabana, where she had her first steady stripping job in 1972. She was thrilled to be a stripper, and she remembers the club with enthusiasm as the kind of place Sinatra might have worked in. There were waiters in red jackets, a uniformed doorman, polished mirror, red flocked wallpaper, a lazy susan laden with bottles of liquor slowly rotating on the bar, and a round stage with a wrought-iron railing.

The manager there was Charlie. He was like an uncle, says Dragu.

He'd run that place for eight years in that location, and Lord knows how many years before that in its old locale. He had short grey hair, a moustache, wore white shirts with the sleeves rolled up, and smoked Export A cigarettes. We sang birthday greetings to him on his birthday – he was well loved.

Charlie was always protecting us from the owner of the club, who came to visit only once in a while, and was out of touch with what was happening there. Charlie knew how we felt – he worked with us every day. The owner didn't understand that we were people. Still, all raises had to come through the owner.

Dragu had been hired by Charlie. She didn't meet the owner until he came for a visit one night after she had been working there a few weeks. He watched Dragu dance, and was delighted. He took her into his office and gave her a raise as a way of encouraging her to stay on at his club. Then Dragu went back to work, and the owner sat down and proceeded to get drunk and enjoy the strippers in his establishment.

In one of her acts, Dragu danced to a song called the "Theme from Shaft." The owner took a fancy to this song, and when she had finished dancing, he immediately called for the song to be played again, and asked Dragu to get back on stage. This was highly unusual. The strippers normally took turns, and varied their music and their acts from set to set. But as the evening advanced, and he became more inebriated, he continued to insist that Dragu dance out of turn to this one song.

"No, no, no! I don't want Simone to dance," he bellowed. "I want Angie to dance. Put on the 'Theme from Shaft'."

The customers were uneasy, and Dragu and the other employees felt embarrassed, but Dragu danced as ordered. She didn't know what else to do. She felt incapable of refusing. In her mind, these favours to the owner were a requirement of the raise he had given her.

She felt like a trained dog, she says. She was wearing a gold chain around her neck that night, and she kept touching it and thinking: "So this is what I have to do to go from $25 to $40 a night. Be willing to dance every time I hear the 'Theme from Shaft'."

Of course, there was an appealing side to these events. There was approval and desire as well as dominance in the owner's behaviour. Patriarchal control betrays a degree of need that creates a secure position for a woman.

Dragu recalls another manager, Dino, who once walked into the dressing room with her week's pay when she had just come off stage. She was sweaty from dancing, and wearing only high heels and a g-string. Dino, in his business suit, handed her a roll of bills, and asked her to count it while he watched. It took Dragu several long minutes to get through the five hundred in twenties, and she enjoyed every bit of it. Although she normally values, and even demands privacy in the dressing room, this incident seemed to her like a titillating scene from a B-movie, in which she was the star.

Dragu once had a terrifying encounter with the same Dino. At that period of her life, she was living in Montreal with another stripper, Claire, and both women were busy with the film "Theatre for Strangers," a documentary about stripping that featured themselves. They were looking for clubs where they could shoot footage for the film. Dino agreed to let them use his club for one day, and as part of the deal, they both agreed to dance there for a week at the usual rate of pay.

They worked at the club for four days, and did their shoot mid week. The next day, they realized they were exhausted, and too busy with the film to be stripping as well. They decided to terminate their week's contract with Dino, but to send him girls to take their places. This was common practice, and so they sent their replacements to the club without first warning him. Claire sent a hippie girlfriend to take over her job as go-go dancer, and Dragu sent a black stripper who had worked for Dino before. But while Dragu and Claire thought that sending substitutes to the club was the responsible thing to do, it seems that Dino perceived it as an appropriation of his authority.

That same day, Dragu went to the club to make sure everything was going as planned, and to collect the money she and Claire were owed for four days of dancing.

I walked into the club mid afternoon. It was practically empty and there was a lazy feeling. The tv was on. The hippie chick Claire had sent was swinging in her go-go cage. She was wearing one of Claire's costumes – a pair of bejewelled lime green bikini panties. Bobbe with the tits was sipping a rum and coke, and she laughed and waved when she saw me.

I was looking around for Dino when he came striding over to me. He looked angry. He stood and faced me. I always spoke English with Dino, but for some reason – I think because I had been speaking French with the film crews and everyone in the clubs during the film shoot – I launched into my explanations to Dino in French. I explained how exhausted Claire and I were, and that the filming was more arduous than we had expected. I apologized for not finishing the week, and said that I hoped he found the hippie topless dancer and the black stripper to be satisfactory. I said that he could pay Claire and I for four days, and the other two girls for the three remaining days.

When I stopped talking, Dino started to scream at me in English.

"Don't condescend to me by speaking to me in French. I speak French to the French girls, and I speak English to the English girls."

He went on screaming, saying that there had already been a black stripper the week before I came and that the customers would complain that all the strippers were black. He told me that he was the one who chose all the girls, and that Claire couldn't send in a friend of hers out of the blue. Suddenly he stopped his tirade to shout:

"I want Claire back! I want Claire back! Send Claire back!"

Then he shrieked: "I'm going to get you blacklisted in all the clubs in Montreal. You are never going to strip in Montreal again."

He waved his hands around and his rage grew and grew. I was frightened, but stood facing him, too scared to move. Suddenly he lifted his right hand to hit me. I was lucky – a customer who had been watching jumped between us, put his hands on Dino's shoulders, and walked him away from me.

Dragu met her patriarchal nemesis towards the end of her years as a stripper. He was a manager called Santo. For Dragu, he was the archetypal boss daddy. She saw him as an icon of power, glowing with strength, authority, and personal magnetism. Her very description of him embodies the depth of her romantic fixation.

He was an attractive, powerful man – six feet tall with dark hair and olive skin. He wore a dark suit and white shirt with the tie loosened, and looked incredibly sexy in this outfit. His world-weary look said that he had been everywhere and done everything, in the style of the gentleman maverick. His big hands were vicelike in fights, but could also reach out tenderly in kindness. He smelled of soap and tobacco. He was smart and sensitive and knew how to run a club. He commanded respect.

Dragu's adulation of Santo extended even to a filial kind of devotion.

Santo used to grin at me proudly and pull me into a big bear hug, the way my papa used to. Pinch my cheeks. He used to watch me dance, and give his approval. I wanted to be his favourite. He wanted me to do him proud.

Santo was a married man who lived in a suburb with his family. He was having an affair of long standing with a stripper called Jean – a redhead known in the club for her exquisite breasts. There were constant rumours that Santo forced strippers to have sex with him in his office, though Dragu says she never believed them because he didn't treat her that way. He did, however, have an evident fetish for black women, and Dragu thought that the rumours about him might contain some truth when it came to black strippers, many of whom were from the Islands and working in Canada illegally. It would have been easy for him to force sexual favours under threat of firing, and possible deportation. There are no direct testimonials, however – just one third-hand story. A waitress who worked for Santo reports that the bartender told her he saw Santo making it with a black stripper in his office. As the bartender passed by the open office door, Santo looked up and laughed at being caught, meanwhile not missing a stroke.

As a stripper, Dragu had a policy of no sex with managers. Although she found many of them attractive, she saw them as roosters, and felt that strippers lost status when they did it with the manager. Managers are easy to fall in love with, Dragu acknowledges, but she did it herself only from a distance.

Dragu first worked for Santo during the summer of '77, on her return to Toronto after touring one of her dance-theatre works across Canada. She liked the women she worked with, and she liked her job. There was a live band, and the musicians and the girls worked well together. The music was excellent, and the atmosphere in the club was hot and inventive. All the strippers were using sparkle dust that summer – gluing it to their bodies and costumes, and throwing it around the stage, laughing at the complaints of the musicians that the stuff was in their instruments, and their pockets and pant cuffs, and even in their beds at home.

During the time Dragu had been away, a bizarre event had completely altered the moral climate of Toronto. A boy had been raped and murdered by two or three men. Because the crime had been done in a Yonge Street building that also housed a brothel, there was a huge public outcry against the sex industries as well as against the gay community. Politicians and moralists launched a so-called "cleanup campaign." Massage parlours cum brothels were closed, prostitutes were carted off to jail, and gays and strippers were harassed in the streets and in clubs. Dragu says that she was constantly stopped and questioned by policemen in the vicinity of the club, until eventually she had the bouncer help her get a taxi each night after work.

The harassment had a strong effect on Dragu, and on others in her position, who were being treated as enemies of the community on the basis of their work or their sexuality. The social ostracism Dragu normally experienced as a stripper was greatly amplified. Thus began an erosion of her morale which was to become devastating for her that summer.

Her troubles became critical when she fell ill with bronchitis, not long after starting her job with Santo. She blamed her illness on a large air conditioner that blasted cold air onto the stage as she danced. It couldn't be shut off, said the manager, because it was there for the comfort of the clientele.

She was not doing well financially. She had moved into an apartment she couldn't afford, but didn't feel free to leave because she had sublet from friends. Taking a week's sick leave from work left her short of money, and she borrowed what she needed from Santo.

It was galling for Dragu to be working six nights a week and living poorly, and yet to be in debt to the manager. To add to her frustration, it was at this time that a local newspaper published a feature article about her, touting her as a dancer, stripper, and philosopher with street-smart appeal. The article, which brought in a lot of business for Santo, mentioned that Dragu's salary was $25 a night. Santo's reaction was: "Why did you tell them what you're really getting? It makes you sound cheap."

He didn't offer her a raise. Just the opposite – he started asking her for favours. She was an easy mark – short of money, afraid of losing her job, and personally in debt to him.

Will you dance in the cellar on your break? I'm short a girl down there. Will you sit with my friends Joseph and Leo – keep them company, show them a good time. Will you work a double on Monday? Lara-Lee is booked off to visit her sick mother-in-law.

He never demanded or threatened, but she felt a real or imagined threat in his cocked eyebrow, his way of looking at her.

Time passed, the requests kept coming, and Dragu continued to comply. Her bronchitis had never fully disappeared. She was exhausted, ill and demoralized. A sense of desperation began to grow in her.

I was on a terrible treadmill. I thought I would die in that club, a slave to the manager. I thought: This is what the rest of my life will be like – slowly dying in front of this air conditioner, and being short of money. I became more and more passive. I had no will. I felt pinned and helpless. The more I complied with his requests, the more I had to comply, like the seam that begins to rip. As time passed, I felt less and less capable of making a move to help myself. I was filled with guilt and fear. I experienced a total loss of perspective.

One evening, Santo asked Dragu to come and see him in his office. She arrived in her between-sets dress – a black polyester evening gown with an elasticized neck trimmed with a flounce that Dragu wore off the shoulder. She sported long, dangling earrings, and wore her hair as she had for her show – swept into a topknot with a plastic rose attached. She was trying for a Spanish look that summer.

Santo's office was like a Hollywood set: faded brocade wall-paper, fake wood panelling, fluorescent lights – one tube burnt out, one glowing, 8 x 10 glossies of girls called Sally Gayle and Pistol Polly tacked to the walls, an old safe in the corner. (Dragu had once been in Santo's office when he was opening the safe. He fiddled with the dial for a while, then sighed and laughed and told her, "I just can't do this in front of you. I know you're not watching, but I'd feel better if you'd turn your back.") A pyramid of butts stood in the ashtray, and there were two old scotch glasses on the desk – one with a butt floating in it, another with the liquor crystallized at the bottom. The bartender will never get it clean was Dragu's thought on entering the room.

She stopped part way to his desk, and waited while he poured scotch into a clean glass. He looked up.

"You want?"

"No."

She took the cigarette he held out and leaned across to let him light it. His attentiveness alerted her that something was up. He even seemed a little shy.

He walked around the desk and stood close to her, playing with the wisps of hair at the back of her neck.

"You're a beautiful dancer," he murmured. "Special. I knew I really liked you the first time I saw you."

The countless seductions he was reputed to have performed might have begun in just this way. Dragu could easily picture him purring around his women, flattering and caressing as he manoeuvred them to sit on his desk, kissing their ears and throats, and gently pushing their thighs apart, persuading them with soft words, without direct threat.

But it wasn't sex he wanted of Dragu.

"I know you have influence with the girls," he breathed.

At some point in the club's history, the girls had all been issued fishnet body stockings, which they wore instead of g-strings. They liked the body stockings because, even though they were transparent, they disguised scars and cellulite, and provided a sense of being clothed. Now Santo wanted them to wear g-strings instead, and they wouldn't, so he was asking Dragu if she would make the switch first, and persuade the others to follow.

He had asked many favours of Dragu, and she had complied without resistance, but for some reason, this request filled her with rage. She says that this, above all else, indicated that he didn't really care about the comfort and welfare of his family of workers. Her anger had not been roused in her own defence, but flared up readily on behalf of the other girls. She refused to co-operate.

This event marked the beginning of a change that ended her entrapment. One more incident – a customer grabbed her thigh from behind while she was dancing – increased her feelings of impotence, but things were beginning to move in her mind. She read a book called *How It All Began* – the memoirs of Bommi Baumann, the West German terrorist. "It made me realize I was not messed up because I was an asshole," she says. "It gave me the strength to see that I was oppressed." Soon afterwards someone offered her a job as an actress in a cabaret. The wages were slightly higher and she was able to pay Santo back the week after she quit working for him. She had been there for four months.

But Dragu felt bored by the cabaret scene. It was, she says, like food without salt. She was still passionately attracted to stripping. As well, her anger and indignation towards Santo and managers and men acted as a magnet, drawing her inevitably back into the conflict.

She worked for Santo again about a year later for a period of nine months. She was in a much stronger position this time. She had achieved something close to star status on the strip circuit. This happened through the continuing press she was receiving for her work as a dancer and performance artist in the civilian world. She now commanded a higher wage as a stripper, and she commanded more respect as well.

Her newfound political awareness changed her attitude to Santo. Seeing herself as an oppressed worker, and as part of a tradition of oppressed workers, made her believe she had a right, even an obligation to provide for herself. As well, her new way of thinking eroded some of her romantic idealization of the patriarch, helping her to view managers more practically.

She now quarrelled with Santo endlessly over working conditions. He was still a romantic figure for her, but she no longer felt an urge to obey him. Argue though she might, however, she made no headway. She says that she felt like the Margaret character in "Dennis the

Menace" comics, making indignant and totally ineffectual complaints with her hands on her hips, and becoming more and more angry as Santo tried to hold her hand and sweet talk her troubles away. It was on this wave of quarrelling with Santo that Dragu finally quit stripping at the end of 1979.

We had one very special conversation towards the end of my days of working with him. We talked about Spain and travelling. It was very close and romantic – we even held hands a little. It was such a wonderful coming together, and yet we would always have to be enemies.

Dragu's feud with Santo embodied the quarrel of the oppressor with the oppressed on many fronts. It was a battle between employer and worker, between man and woman, between parent and child. It was both political and personal – a battle of issues and a battle of wills. Dragu felt that moral right was with her, but that she had little or no power to get what she wanted.

After she quit stripping, Dragu began working with Bridget, who was facing a nudity charge at the time. Together, they investigated strippers' rights through meetings with the CLC, ACTRA, the Civil Liberties Association, and Legal Aid. Dragu also did interviews and debates for radio and TV. She had seen that her personal dilemma was based in problems that existed independently of her own involvement in them. Now she could enlist the support of the group and the legal system to provide the clout that she lacked as an individual.

Yet Dragu still carried a belief in her own powerlessness, even as she engaged in the fight for rights. As so often happens, the righteous anger that fueled her political activism was based in a sense of impotence.

Powerlessness may be learned by experience, but once it becomes part of an individual's identity, it tends to create feelings and experiences that prove its veracity. This is to say that when you perceive those you are bargaining with as having all the power, you do not expect to make important gains, and you are not likely to. Conversely, an individual who feels an innate sense of personal power will not be cast in powerless roles. It is important to realize this because once a belief in one's own impotence has been accepted, nothing can essentially change until the issue is faced within the self. The power of the group may override the personal limitations of its members, but will not alter them.

Dragu's relationship with Santo is strikingly similar to Cindy's relationship with Nick. In both cases, the women gave away their power. Dragu says that she felt the urge to obey Santo, in spite of his making no actual threats of demands. But even Dragu's eventual realization that she could assert herself did not resolve her problem – it merely brought her to a different stage of the power struggle. She continued to feel quite as powerless as she did before, only now she was actively angry about it. She quarrelled with Santo over working conditions, but got nowhere. He still had all the power, and in a purely psychological sense, that fit Dragu's schemata at the time. She believed that the world was polarized into the powerful and the powerless, and that bosses and men had the power. She learned to see the world in those terms long before her meeting with Santo.

The patriarch can exist only in relation to the child-woman. The two roles create and animate one another. He is entrapped by his role just as she is by hers. He is subject to the acquired sense that he must control and dominate in order to invest himself with authority, just as she is subject to her sense of herself as weak and in need of male approbation. It is a pas de deux, and in order for it to continue, each person must keep within the prescribed configuration. There is no denying that many of us have been drilled in the steps of this dance from birth, yet at some point, each person must begin to take responsibility for his or her own motion.

X

GIRLS GIRLS
GIRLS
GREAT PIZZA
920
ADULT ENTERTAINMENT
LICENCED by L.L.B.O.

Getting Down with the Boys

Striptease is a thriving business in many places throughout the world. In Canada, it is so popular that most of us can see it by making the short trip to a local tavern. Striptease persists despite its enemies and its bad reputation. Men want strippers and they always have. Why they do is a question that mystifies many women. Strippers themselves don't know for sure why men want to watch them. They offer opinions, but usually indicate they are only guessing.

Bridget says that a strip club is a man's only refuge from feminists. Interest in a woman on a purely sexual basis is accepted in clubs. Even so, Bridget adds, most men do not relate to strippers lasciviously. She talks about the audience at Le Strip – the Toronto strip club that is set up like a theatre and doesn't sell liquor. The same men have been going there for years, she says, and they always sit in the same seats, just like in school or in church. Bridget says she could point to each one blindfolded: Clifford, Bill, Tokyo Joe, the guy who claps all the time, the guy who jerks off all the time and the guy with the funny belly-button who opens his shirt. They feel paternal towards her, not sexual, she believes. She used to think they wanted only to look at her naked body, so one night she went on without a costume and danced her whole set completely nude. They hated it. Now she thinks they want eye contact more than anything else. If she looks at them, they're happy.

Gwendolyn believes men come to the club because it's their hangout. The stripper is there merely to help pass the time. Gwendolyn promotes the safety-valve theory – if a guy has a fight with his wife, he can have a few drinks and spew out a bit of venom at the stripper. She adds that some men are sexually excited by the idea that strippers are women who are degrading themselves. Like Bridget, Gwendolyn believes that most customers want her attention more than anything else.

The odd collection of customers at Le Strip has also come under Gwendolyn's scrutiny. She tells the story of a man in the audience who was wearing dark glasses, humming to the music, and not watching her show. She figured he wanted attention, so she went over to his side of the stage and asked him to take off her shoe. When he got the shoe off he handed it to her and made a grab at her thigh. She subdued him by smacking his head with the shoe, and then went on with her show. But as she came off stage, one of the girls said to her: "Gwendolyn! You were beating up a blind man!" And Gwendolyn said, "Oh my God! That's why he was wearing sunglasses. That's why he wasn't looking at me." But then the other girls said, "Oh that's just Blind Joe. He isn't really blind. He gets out his cane and sunglasses at the bottom of the stairs on his way in."

Jamie of Vancouver says that men come to strip clubs because they don't otherwise get a chance to look at nude women, especially so many different ones.

Fonda Peters says there are as many reasons as there are different kinds of noses. College kids, she says, come in for a laugh – they're cocksure and a bit embarrassed and try to outdo one another in what they can yell at the stripper. The young executives have chips on their shoulders and aren't sure of their manhood, and they come to the club to insult the strippers and order them about. Men on pensions and welfare spend time in clubs because they have nothing else to do. Fonda has dubbed this bunch the Raincoat Brigade, and she says they are charming and fun and like strippers who have plenty of chutzpah.

Jeannie says men come to clubs to relax and be entertained.

Debbie is big on the safety-valve theory. If we didn't have strip clubs, she declares, we'd have more rapes and child abuse. Strip clubs are for men who are lonely or perverted.

Denese says men have told her the cheap beer and free show is the reason they're there, but she thinks the real story is that they want something kinky that the women they're dating won't provide, even if it's as simple as garters and stockings. Men occasionally approach her to say they've always wanted to make it with a black woman, which suggests to her that they spend time in clubs to court their unfulfilled fantasies.

Morgana says men come to see strippers because they're fighting with their wives or because they're sexually bored, or both.

There is probably some truth in all of these views and yet they have no cohesion. At the time when Dragu and I were asking strippers these questions, I couldn't understand what men saw in strippers, and found that the collective answers of the strippers didn't clarify anything for me. On the whole, they seemed like a pot-luck hash, haphazardly conceived and lacking something essential.

While I was thinking over this problem, a writer friend of Dragu's called Paul came back from a trip to Germany with a story that I found interesting because it was so perplexing. The story he told was about visiting a club in Berlin. It was a chilly late fall and he was in the city on business and feeling lonely and disoriented. One night, after wandering around by himself for most of the day and then going to a movie, he went into a club that advertised strippers. He sat down at the bar and was immediately accosted by a B-girl. He describes her as plump and blonde and wearing a green halter dress. Her name was Marianna. She wanted to cuddle and talk, and she encouraged Paul to buy a small bottle of champagne to share with her. He didn't find her particularly attractive, he says, but he was curious about her life. She had lived in Texas for five years with an American husband, then left her husband and brought her children home to Germany. Paul wondered how she had ended up hustling men in a Berlin club.

He enjoyed the talk and the intimacy. The liquor and the sensuous atmosphere began to relax him. He bought more champagne at her suggestion. They moved from the bar to a table, and then to an enclosed booth. Marianna sat with her leg thrown across Paul's lap and talked constantly. She objected to the flow of immigrants into

Berlin. He didn't like her politics. Even so, he bought more and more champagne. She wanted him to take off his shirt. He resisted, until finally he said okay, if she would do the same. So he took off his shirt, and she let down the top of her halter dress. She encouraged him to touch and fondle her, but she was not available for sex. He stayed long into the night, and when he finally decided it was time to go, he found he had spent $300 on champagne. He later referred to the experience as the night he lost his shirt.

In telling the story, Paul said he was annoyed about the money because he had to move to a cheaper hotel, but he claimed not to regret the experience, admitted no animosity towards Marianna, and insisted that he had not felt duped or manipulated in the least, but had played his part willingly because he was interested in the experience for its own sake. His attitude seemed outrageous to me. It was obvious that he had made a bad deal. I couldn't understand him at all.

I was once surprised to hear Dragu come out with the old saying: Men only want one thing. When she said it, I laughed and told her it applied to her more than any of the men I knew. I had never thought of men that way, or so I believed until I started thinking about Paul's story and why it unsettled me. It occurred to me that I would have been content with the story and with Paul's attitude if only he had got laid. If Paul had made it with the B-girl, then I would have agreed that he hadn't completely wasted his money, and thus had no reason for regret. Because, after all, there is a tradition of sex being something men pay for.

Close behind that thought came the understanding I had been looking for. I knew why it had made no sense to me that men spend time watching strippers. I had been harbouring a deep conviction that men wanted sexual intercourse above all else – that they were not interested in anything subtle or romantic or merely titillating – that they only tolerated that sort of dallying when they couldn't get the real thing, or as a necessary lead-in to the real thing. I believed that men's sexuality was one-dimensional. I believed that men only wanted one thing. And if men were after sex and little else, what in the world are they doing in strip clubs? Watching strippers does not provide men with opportunities to have sex. In fact, watching strippers is an abdication of the pursuit of sex, since most men are not doing it with strippers, and women on the make don't hang around strip clubs, and prostitutes have their own places – sometimes strip clubs, sometimes not.

That was a turning point for me. My dissatisfaction disappeared, and I began to accept at face value the variety of reasons people were offering for men's interest in strippers. There could be no single right answer because every man was different.

Ralph and the 600 Ethnics

Ralph is an actor. Ralph doesn't like the word "fat" used around him in any context whatsoever. He is quite portly – I think very attractive in a round way. He has lively eyes and is tremendously funny – very observant of mankind. And a very good actor. Ralph and Ivan, another friend, made a movie together in which they both played terrorists. You should have seen how Ralph got shot and how he died. He died so well.

According to Ivan, Ralph is wired to porno. Ralph says he gave it up – just found it sad one day and quit going. But when he liked it, he liked peep shows best – the Times Square variety. He talks about how laws come and go – there used to be no partitions between the girl and the men, and it could get really wild, he says, depending on the girl. Sometimes there would be lots of guys sucking her off. Then the cops came and closed it down and the action moved on to something else.

Ralph expressed an interesting wish that strippers be funnier. He would like to go to a strip club and see an act that mixed comedy and sex.

The last time he saw a strip show, which was just a week before I interviewed him, was at the Metro on Bloor Street. At the time, the Metro alternated strippers and porn movies, though now it's down to one stripper per night. Anyway, Ralph had an amazing experience there and was so excited when he told me about it that he jumped up out of his seat.

He had gone in and the place was packed with men. Six hundred, he claims. And the stripper, in very bright lights, started to dance and strip, and when she took off her g-string and spread her legs to show her pussy, the men stood up and clapped, very seriously. "Like this!" said Ralph, and he showed me. Solemn and urgent, with great respect. He felt the men were saying they appreciated and respected her courage in showing her cunt.

Nothing received applause except this. He said he was the only non ethnic there. He felt like an alien – one Jew in this Toronto Pussy Palace for Catholics. He felt he had walked in on a secret religious ceremony: Goddess stripper performs illegal but sacred rites for six hundred men. It would be scorned outside these walls, but was adored inside the shrine. They revered this woman for doing something they would kill their wives for doing. I wondered afterwards if Ralph, as an actor, might have felt a sense of shared experience with the stripper as she received her standing ovation.

The Collector

Carl is in his forties, an artist in Vancouver, and classically handsome. He looks like Peter Gunn or The Spirit. He loves B-movies and jazz music, fifties culture cum sex and violence, nightclub glamour and naughty things. He collects pornography in the form of pictures, video, super 8 and magazines.

Carl has a magnetic power to lure people into his land of obsessions. So intense is his desire that his associates gladly act out his fantasies with him and for him. One friend simulated heroin injections into her thigh while wearing only a bikini bottom – for Carl's camera. Another gave Carl an off-camera hand job with hand lotion while Carl lay nude on a couch fondling his gun. People who would normally say no to such activities are overwhelmed by Carl's enjoyment and understanding of his chosen fetishes.

I worked as an actress for Carl once, in a videotape based on the B-film-style cartoon comics that he has been drawing since he was eleven. We shot five minutes of me rubbing my thighs and panties with a gun. The scene was never used for the videotape. Did I mention that Carl is obsessive? The cameraperson finally said, "I really think that's enough Carl. We have used a lot of tape on this."

Carl is frankly obsessed with cunt. He says he "collects" it – all races and ages and personalities of cunt. Pictures mainly, but that's not all. An artist friend of mine reports that she met Carl for the first time when she looked him up to borrow a slide projector for a performance she was doing in Vancouver. She invited him to the show, and he came back stage two minutes before showtime – to the bathroom she was using as a dressing room. She was just fixing her lipstick when he came in and asked if he could first look at and then taste her pussy for his collection. He was gracious and even reverent, she reports, as if he was asking to see a beautiful work of art. She figured it was okay since she had no time to discuss it. Besides, she had heard from another travelling artist that Carl had done this to her on her visit to Vancouver.

When I was in Vancouver doing the promotional tour for the movie "Surfacing," I interviewed Carl about strippers. He has no clear idea about the difference between stripping and hooking. Everything clouds over in his love of pussy. He wants a little look. Give me a little peek, a little look-see.

He loved the peep shows he went to in Times Square when he was in New York. Especially the kind where he got to tell the stripper what he wanted her to do. He asked her to show him her cunt, he says, and he got so excited when she did that he nearly came in his pants.

Carl doesn't spend a lot of time in strip clubs – he wishes they were more sophisticated and exclusive. But strippers enact some of his best-loved fantasies. He adores stockings and garter belts and long gloves with jewels on them and corsets and uplift brassières. He dotes on the idea that a woman could step out of a long dress and be wearing all that underneath, and he could make love to her in that.

His all-time favourite stripper was a classically fifties lady he saw in Vancouver. She was from the old school of false eyelashes and wig and getting down with the boys, as Carl puts it, which means she came down off the stage and mixed with the customers during her act. Her armpits were shaved and she was totally plastic looking, he recalls with pleasure.

Carl really hates the hippie strippers. It's not just that their aesthetic doesn't please him – the leg and armpit hair and the athletic approach to stripping done with no costume to speak of. It's that they have no respect for the legacy of courtesans, for the symbols and the mysteries, and the elevation of sexuality that is the history of the stripper. Carl wants pussy but he wants it with a certain aesthetic and ritual.

He despises the other men in strip clubs. They're crude, he says, and they spoil his experience. He would like to watch strippers in a more refined atmosphere, with men who have more respect. I agree with Carl that strip clubs can be guilty of catering to base sexuality or the lowest common denominator of taste. Carl's taste in sexuality is tailored, refined and esoteric, with history behind it – just like his taste in music and art. To Carl, sex is one of the finer things in life.

The Accountant

I met Clive at a Board of Directors' Meeting for an arts organization. It was a hot summer day. Clive swung his jacket over the back of a chair and loosened his tie. He was wearing a crisp, short-sleeved white shirt and was very tanned. He is semi-bald, wears glasses and has a soft voice. He is very attractive and looks healthy.

Clive is an accountant with a large firm of chartered accountants. That summer I was looking for the reasonable man's opinion of strippers. This man, I thought, is an established professional with an interest in the arts – he is sure to be reasonable. I asked him if he ever watched strippers. He was surprised to be asked this question, but yes, he did, and yes, he was willing to talk.

Clive usually sees strippers with a gang of other accountants after work. Strippers provide a backdrop and a stimulus for conversation. The accountants eat and drink and wonder if the stripper is a good lay or, if she is athletic, they speculate on her repertoire of love-making positions. Clive is particularly fond of athletic strippers. He says: "I like a well-tuned body. I find women athletes have an erotic quality." He finds short-shorts an exciting costume. Even running shoes and a singlet. He likes flesh and muscle and a minimum of fat.

Clive is very into bodies and body parts. He talks about "nice legs," a "nice ass," "nice boobs" – he likes small ones. Stripper-watching for him is like browsing in a department store – third-floor bums, second-floor backwards-and-over floor shows highlighting legs and leg warmers. Strippers are a pure spectacle for Clive. He is without fantasies or romantic notions. He just likes looking at bodies.

Clive married a woman of the physical type he most admires – a modern dancer with a well-tuned, athletic body. Strippers are not giving him something he can't get at home. They don't offer forbidden charms or exotic flavours. Watching strippers is entertainment, pure and simple – a chance to unwind after work.

When I first talked to Clive, I thought: A perfectly reasonable man. Maybe he's right, and stripping is no more complicated than a moving backdrop of pleasing bodies. But I eventually decided that Clive's answers were no more right than anyone else's. I was relieved to come to this conclusion because I wasn't quite comfortable with Clive's conviction that strippers are "unambitious". For Clive, there is nothing sleazy or immoral about stripping, but a stripper is "capitalizing on a very temporal thing, which is her physical beauty," and that, he believes, is unambitious.

The Insider

Jack is a lively, blonde, kind of jive-ass white guy – sensuous and a good talker. He's an artist and musician. Back in the seventies, he used to work as a bartender and a bar musician and hang around with strippers. He once went to Kirkland Lake with a stripper who had a gig at a hotel there. Jack and the stripper shared a room upstairs, and he used to help her dress for her show. It was like harnessing a horse, he says, because her costumes were theatrical and old-fashioned, with lots of strange fastenings. This woman couldn't dance, but she stripped in the grand tradition, and that's what Jack loves in a stripper – stockings and garters and long gloves and all that paraphernalia, and a woman who knows the traditional burlesque moves. He is not fetishistic about strippers, he says, but he does admire a stripper as he would a race horse – for her style and elegance.

Strippers are not erotic for Jack in a general way. He doesn't deny occasionally getting an erection watching them, but correlates that reaction with feelings of excitement that are not necessarily sexual. He says that when he was a kid in school he used to get erections in history class if the lesson was interesting. More recently, he was turned on watching folk dancers in Bali because the music and dancing were beautiful. Jack says that if he gets an erection for a stripper, it's a real compliment to her.

He talks about the moment at the end of a show when a stripper gathers up her clothes and leaves the stage. He finds that the most interesting part of the dance because it's then that the stripper reveals how she feels about her work. He likes to know strippers. He talks to them when he can, and sometimes gets to know them, and sometimes thinks he would like to make love to them. He relates to them as an insider because he's worked in nightclubs and knows what that's all about. But approaching a stripper as an outsider – as a male customer – doesn't provide opportunities to develop a personal relationship with her, and so there is an element of frustration for Jack in watching strippers.

It's interesting that Jack is the only man Dragu and I interviewed who said he would like to make love to some of the strippers he watched, and even so, he qualified that as coming from a feeling of kinship and affection based on his roots as a worker and performer in nightclubs.

When Jack said he classifies strippers as artists, he pleased Dragu, who has long been trying to persuade people that strippers are artists. Jack is quite firm on this point and says the reason people don't think of strippers as artists is the division in our culture between highbrow and lowbrow. Jack doesn't consider any one art form to be better or higher than any other. He sees stripping as decorative art, or folk art, but doesn't rate it lower than other kinds of art.

And since stripping is art, Jack would like to see it go the way of other art forms and adopt more political content. He suggests as possibilities: stripping to a recorded speech by Leon Trotsky or Malcolm X; stripping out of a blue Chinese worker's suit with Maoist props; stripping to a song by Clive Robertson, who combines a disco beat with boy-Marxist lyrics.

Undoubtedly stripping would be more creative, more political, and more individual if it weren't for the rigid performance standards dictated by club owners, who fire strippers for the slightest deviation from convention.

Consumer with a Conscience

Matt is married and in his early thirties. He is tall, blonde and blue-eyed with a collegiate look – corduroy pants and button-down shirts. Matt comes from a family that was involved in criminal activities. When he was a kid, his mother, who has an Irish criminal background, used to work as a prostitute and drive getaway cars. His grandmother had worked as a prostitute in her day. His father made money from safecracking, armed robbery, bootlegging, fencing and booze cans.

Matt was made a ward of the state at age two, and spent much of his childhood in group and foster homes in Southern Ontario. He went to a total of thirty-two public schools, he says. As a teenager, he was frequently in trouble with the law and spent time in reform schools. But Matt was smart, and did well in school. He went to University and got a BA and now works with computers.

Stripping is not a big part of Matt's life. He goes to clubs every now and then, often with his co-workers who visit clubs to get their minds off work. He doesn't stay long because there isn't enough variety. After one or two strippers it's like reading a magazine you've just finished reading – there are no surprises, he says, because the routine is always the same. But he does go.

His interest in strippers is purely sexual. For Matt, strippers perform a sexual service and that's it. He does not see them as dancers and performers, and he certainly doesn't believe they are artists. Matt goes to a strip club for cheap thrills. Strippers enact some of his sexual fantasies, get his juices flowing, give him an erection. Matt always gets an erection watching strippers. In fact, he can't imagine a stripper who wouldn't give him an erection.

Not that he doesn't have preferences. Although he believes all women are potentially erotic, he likes his strippers slender, well-proportioned, and without scars, bruises, tattoos, or any kind of disfigurement. He wants strippers who seem to be in control of their appearance and who show enthusiasm for their work. These things are important because they indicate that the stripper has made a conscious choice to do what she is doing, and Matt then doesn't have to worry that he is helping to perpetuate her victim status. Matt has two sisters who have worked as strippers – one has been a battered wife and the other is involved with drugs and prostitution as well as stripping. Matt associates stripping with pornography, prostitution, drugs, violence, and a bad start in life, and he thinks that most women who work as strippers or hookers are victims of circumstance – women who have no other way of getting money and who are not in control of their lives. He wonders if it's actually possible for a woman to make a conscious, objective choice to be a stripper. If a stripper looks like she's having a bad time up there on stage, Matt starts to think he's one of the people responsible for her misery.

Matt's conscience designs his preferences, but doesn't keep him away. He likes and wants sexual entertainment. He finds it frustrating that you can't see good pornography in Toronto. He would like to see high-quality video pornography with good story lines. No s&m. He has no particular taste for raunchy stuff, but he likes novelty, and novelty usually means whatever the law is suppressing. He points out that if the law required that strippers always wear socks, he would be interested in seeing a stripper without socks. This, he says, is largely a reaction against censorship, which makes him think he's missing something.

Cheap thrills is Matt's easy reason for seeking out strippers, but on another level, he thinks stripping is an amazing phenomenon. When we think about interaction between men and women, he says, we don't think about striptease, and yet stripper-to-audience relationships are common and widespread. A woman standing nude before a room full of men is bizarre when you think about it, but it happens every day, all over the world.

Thoroughly Modern Gilles

Gilles is a teacher, photographer and single father. I have known him for years and regard him as the new modern man – he thinks of himself as a mother. Originally from Arkansas, Gilles came to Canada as a draft dodger and settled in Toronto. He raises two boys and shares a house with a long-time friend who is an actor.

Gilles is tall, slender, good looking and has an extremely deep voice. Because of his voice and height, he can seem tough and imposing but he is a very sensitive and vulnerable man. He loathes violence. He was beaten as a child by both his parents. Violence makes him ill.

One of the first times Gilles invited me to his house for dinner, the bedtime story he read to his two sons was Bukowski's piece about a stripper he had seen as an underager. The two boys explained that Bukowski was their favourite author at the moment. This choice of reading material was my introduction to Gilles' unique child-raising methods.

Like Bukowski, Gilles was introduced to stripping as an underager. It was in St. Louis, Missouri when he was sixteen. The stripper was Evelyn, with her $50,000 treasure chest insured by Lloyd's of London. She was old and not erotic, Gilles recalls. But he liked the comics. They told lewd jokes which he repeated to his friends, and that made him a hit. Two prostitutes tried to pick him up at the *burlesque palace. They asked him to help them move some furniture, but when he arrived at their apartment there wasn't any furniture to be moved. He left puzzled, and it wasn't until three days later that he realized what had been going on.*

The first time Gilles saw a stripper and liked her was in Chicago in 1969 during the bird-cage craze. Remember those women suspended in swinging cages over bars, stripping and go-going? Gilles describes himself at that time as being very uptight about sex. He tried to look without letting people notice he was looking. Did he get a hard-on? "I'd get a sort of quarter mast."

Now Gilles' favourite strippers have nice bodies ("I love looking at a nice pair of breasts."), look intelligent ("The dumb look never does anything for me."), and most important of all, they can really dance. Even if a stripper is really good looking, if she can't dance he finds it sad. But fascinating. Watching a stripper who dances badly is like looking at a car accident. It rivets him even though it makes him queasy.

One day Gilles called me up and said something terrible had happened to him and could I come over. I went right away and found him pale and sick to his stomach. The evening before, he'd had an argument with his girlfriend and he'd gone to the Concord Tavern to cool out. That's his regular drinking spot. It's a two-floor setup: upstairs beer and tv; downstairs beer, snack bar and strippers. Gilles ran into the stripper briefly at the snack bar telling the woman behind the counter that stripping is just like other kinds of showbiz – if you do it too much, you burn out. That's why she didn't work every night.

Gilles had a beer upstairs and then went downstairs to drink another beer and watch the stripper, who turned out to be a great dancer and very sexy. This stripper wasn't thinking about Kalamazoo Michigan, says Gilles. She made plenty of eye contact, and had a generous spirit and good rock'n'roll music. But suddenly, mid show, she stopped dancing and said:

"This man is throwing ice at me."

She pointed to a young man in a leather jacket, and then turned to the bartender and demanded that he do something about it. The bartender just stood and looked at her. At that point Gilles realized there was a lot of ice on the stage and was surprised he hadn't noticed it before.

The stripper stayed cool but finally said, "One of you spoils it for the rest of you," and started putting her clothes on. The men in the audience jeered. The bartender turned on the tv.

Gilles looked at the man who had thrown the ice. The man's mouth was open – he looked vaguely like an animal. Gilles felt hostile towards him, and was sure the other men did too. He stood up and said:

"Goddammit, help her!"

Everybody turned and looked at him.

"Help her out," he said.

Suddenly Gilles felt his scarf being pulled tight around his neck. Next thing he knew, he was on his back on the floor with a cowboy boot resting on his face. Just resting there. He froze, thinking he was about to be kicked in the head, maybe beaten and killed.

He can't remember exactly what happened next, just that he had a chance to get up, and he did. He got his stuff and went to the door, then realized he'd left his wallet on the table and had to go back for it. He looked around for the stripper but couldn't find her. On the upper level of the tavern he overheard two guys talking.

"What happened to the stripper?"

"Oh, she's just a windup crybaby."

"Yeah, she really fucked up. She ran out crying apparently."

Gilles realized the cool front the stripper had kept up was just for the stage. She'd made a good job of it, but she broke down before she got out of there. He had read the situation accurately.

He wanted to talk to the stripper about what had happened. He went home and got his bike and rode along Bloor Street looking for her, but he didn't find her.

Gilles realizes now that it was within the accepted code of that particular group of men to abuse the stripper, and that he was naive to assume they would side with him. He thinks he should have known better, especially considering his history. He has a strong adverse effect on macho types. "I've had encounters with them all my life," he says. "Growing up in Arkansas, it was difficult to get through a day on the playground without getting the shit kicked out of me. I used to hang out with the girls cause I liked them better."

Thornton Wilder says violence is the result of a lack of imagination. Gilles could imagine what the stripper was feeling – the other men could not. Gilles remembers the beatings at home, being caught in the hostility between his parents. At the Concord Tavern he was caught in the hostility between the audience and the stripper.

The Appreciative Capitalist

Peter is a real-estate developer and a kind, loving father. His favourite book is "Zen and the Art of Motorcycle Maintenance," a book about a man and his son crossing America – just like Peter and his son Kevin going through life. Peter is very blonde and good looking and keeps in shape with karate classes.

I have known Peter for years as the boyfriend of a woman friend. I get on with him very well. Most people get on well with him because he has the ability to stay himself whether he is talking to accountants or zambone drivers.

Peter thinks stripping is sexy. The sexiest thing about it, he says, is a stripper enjoying the feedback from the audience. If she is appreciated and enjoying the appreciation, that's sexy. It's naive to watch a strip show believing the woman on stage wants to have sex with you, says Peter, but if she can remind you what it's like to be desired, that's hot. Knowing the moves is not what counts – for stripping to work, there has to be communication.

Daring is a quality Peter admires in a stripper. He remembers watching Lily St. Cyr at the Victory in 1962 – she was doing the classic stocking bit with a difference. She lay down on her chaise longue, peeled off a stocking, and catapulted it into the air so it floated down onto a clothes tree. That impressed Peter, but what impressed him even more was that she did it again with the other stocking. She knew it couldn't always work, and took the chance of falling flat on the second try.

Peter likes the fact that strippers exist for his (and other men's) pleasure. Anything that's done to please you is a nice thing to have happen, he says. Peter likes to be pleased: good wine, good food, good company, good business deals. He feels no guilt about going to a strip club to be wrapped in pleasure. And sex. Yes sex. Being in a strip club is a relief, he feels, because it's a place where sex is acknowledged, and that makes him feel comfortable and thrilled. Thrilled? How thrilled, I wonder. I want to ask him if he gets an erection watching strippers, but for some reason I feel shy with this man.

"Do you get horny?" I ask.

Peter throws back his head and laughs delightedly. I try again.

"Do you get wet?"

"Me, get wet?" he laughs deeply. I'm laughing too.

"I mean do you get an erection." I say finally.

"Oh yes," he answers, still laughing. He explains that he doesn't get one all the time but sometimes he does. After all, stripping is about sex. It isn't poetry, it isn't art, it's all about glands and secretions and gonads and stuff.

Peter enjoys a wide range of striptease styles. He was thrilled by a stripper in Fort Lauderdale who was really raunchy: she could pick up paper money with the lips of her vagina. A travelling businessman from Cleveland put a ten dollar bill between his teeth and this stripper took the bill out of the guy's mouth with her labia, to the total delight of the businessman from Cleveland and all his buddies. And the total delight of Peter.

As Peter explains how great this act was, I feel silly about my usual reaction to the wiggling, squiggling, serpent strippers who can blow out matches, smoke cigarettes and play the oboe with their pussies. I'm always a bit defensive seeing these things because I think I must match them or follow suit in some way. Peter's good-natured enjoyment of these raunchy shows makes me feel prudish and silly. But he is also open to other kinds of shows. He equally enjoyed a young Vancouver stripper who simply "took off all her clothes and danced and jumped about with a lot of girlish charm and exuberance."

Peter describes a strip show he saw recently in Calgary. He went to a Stampede Breakfast at the Calgary Inn – a huge, downtown hotel right on the swank 4th Avenue hookers' alley (These girls wear furs!). People lined up at 3:30 in the morning, and at 7 a.m. they let in all 1500 of them. There was a big buffet breakfast including garbage pails full of gin and orange juice. By 8:30 they'd gone through three bands and two very raunchy standup comics, and all 1500 of them were roasted. Then, blackout, and a spotlight on one stripper. She was really good, says Peter – a good dancer. Finally, she was dancing in just a tiny g-string in her spotlight, when suddenly there were two spotlights. A man in a cape and black leather outfit appeared. He stripped and danced with the female stripper and the crowd went wild. Peter loved it, and observed they were tremendous-

ly brave and had terrific control of the audience. The crowd was dangerous, he thought. "This wasn't a few drunken rubbies at the Victory. These were 1500 gin-crazed Calgarians at 8:30 in the morning!"

Peter's first strip show ever was at the Victory when he was seventeen. He was shocked but pleased at the respect the men in the audience showed the strippers. They called the girls by pet names like Princess. "Come on Princess, you do it." Peter has been a happy and respectful customer ever since. He feels no guilt about being a stripper fan. He doesn't see stripping as sexist or degrading. And he is glad that male strippers have arrived. He hopes their growing popularity means that women are through pretending they don't like sex and are learning to enjoy men as sex objects. He thinks it would be thrilling to be treated like a sex object.

Because Peter has been watching strippers since 1962 and has been a successful businessman for almost as long, I had to ask him if he thought stripping was dying, replaced by other entertainments like porno films, or just what. He was reassuring.

"I have faith in the market system," he says. "If people want to see strippers, they will be around."

Society thought prostitution and marriage would become obsolete because of the Pill – that we would have a sexual revolution that would leave those two popular institutions behind in the dust. But they are still around. As the continental French say: "Plus ça change, plus ça la même chose."

XI

At the Shrine of the Stripper

Stripping is not a celebrated art form or a flaunted element of culture. If it is culture at all, it is back-street culture. If it is art, it is bad art, or perhaps half art, to correspond to the demi monde from which it springs, and the half light in which it thrives. There is nothing noble or inspiring about sexual exhibits. Everyone knows they belong in carnival sideshows and beer halls – places inhabited by those without sophistication or refinement – by derelicts and the dispossessed.

Why then, do people – journalists mainly – continue to complain that striptease has no artistic merit? Why is striptease forever being exposed as art-less? How many times can a thing be dragged into the light? It seems there is an expectation, perpetually disappointed though it may be, for sex shows to measure up in some way – to be artistic – to be, in some sense, art.

"Sex Not Art," is the usual criticism, and it is often phrased in just this way, as if sex and art were opposites, or if not opposites, then elements on a sliding scale where more of one creates less of the other. Given this system, it is impossible that sex could ever become art or embody art.

The idea that sex precludes art is a very well-established tenet of western thought. Culture may toy with sex from one century to the next, but sex has never been allotted cultural status of its own. Sex is culture's disinherited ancestor, admitted to refined circles only if strictly chaperoned by classical mythology or romantic gentility or some social issue or other. And yet, though it is plain that sex can't be art, there have always been attempts to justify sex shows or give them class by arting them up in some way. Usually this means an application of art prototypes.

For instance, Living Statuary was a popular sex-show format in England and France from the Victorian era into the twenties. Nudes were tolerated on stage if they were stationary, in imitation of art, namely statues. Even better, the nudes were often theatrically arrayed to represent a famous painting or a trumped-up scene from mythology, for instance, "Diana Preparing for the Chase." (Boudoir scenes were popular because they provided the excuse for nudity.) Even today, the classics bear the official, reassuring stamp of art, as I discovered looking at some photos taken by a photography student in a classroom setup. The nude female model was actually holding an urn on her shoulder.

There is a beautiful irony in such charades. They are necessary in the first place because of the premise that sex precludes art. But the same premise makes it impossible for us to believe in them. The artistic references sit on the sexual content like a crown on a beggar – not fooling anybody, but helping us to pretend that what is happening is not really sex.

People who wish to discredit sexual entertainment often resort to the unspoken premise that sex precludes art. They demonstrate that a display is not art, and conclude that it must therefore be sex. When stripper Bridget was tried on a charge of nudity in 1979, the Crown Counsel pointed out that Bridget had never trained in ballet or danced in a ballet performance. He hoped to reveal that her guilt was implicit in this fact through a sort of schoolboy logic in which ballet is synonymous with art.

An interesting twist to this kind of thinking shows up whenever there is sex in legitimate theatre or in art galleries. The sex is "gratuitous," people say. The artistic format is a disguise or a ruse. Somebody is trying to get away with something.

Why people feel the urge to cover up sex is a question that is answered in the accusation itself. It is, after all, never art that is accused of gratuity. "Picasso retrospective cheap display of gratuitous art," is a story we will never have to read.

It is sad that in all of this fuss there is no real concern about art. The issue is obviously not a love of art, but a horror of sexuality. There is, likewise, no genuine interest in stripping, which is rarely judged on any valid basis. The thing that makes stripping good or bad is the sexual representation itself – its style, quality, depth, subtlety, complexity, sophistication. The problem with sex shows is not that they are sexual, but that they so often cheapen or belittle sexuality. It is the particular job of strippers to represent sexuality to the rest of the world, and the only shame is that they so often do it poorly, diminishing sex instead of celebrating it. Not that the stripper is solely responsible. The situation is inevitable, sex being the black sheep of a complacent cultural family. Everybody gets a little sly and shifty when sex walks into the performance arena. Many people look the other way, and the rest don't expect or demand excellence. The surprise is that there are many strippers who transcend the general expectation – many more than you would expect to find in the circumstances.

Sometimes men approach Dragu to tell her about a stripper seen in the past and remembered. One man, the director of a theatre company, was in northern Ontario touring a stage show, and one night went to a tavern with some of the crew. In the tavern there was a drunk who everybody noticed because he was so loud and obnoxious. There was a great deal of astonishment in the room when the drunk got up on stage and transformed himself from a redneck in hardhat, workboots and flannel shirt into an attractive woman. The theatre director was especially impressed by the stripper's acting.

A similar story comes from a Vancouver journalist who was eating lunch one day at Gary Taylor's and noticed a woman who looked like a legal secretary sitting alone at a table. She was wearing a grey skirt, white blouse and glasses, with her hair tied back primly. He thought she seemed out of place sitting by herself at lunchtime. He says:

"Then her set came up. She walked through the crowd and, much to the surprise of myself and anyone else who had noticed her sitting there, got up on stage and ceased to be a legal secretary. She had chosen to adopt a fantasy persona to set up the strip because she had obviously worked it out that at Taylor's on Granville Street at noontime, she was playing to your basic business audience. And that the receptionist they had passed without quite noticing her on the way out of the office suddenly gets up in the middle of lunch and starts to take off her clothes – wow!"

Stripping has a certain potency that is purely visual. Women's bodies and body parts have become iconic in our world, and their display in the flesh is compelling. Inevitably, each of us responds to some version of the icon – a certain style of dress or movement, or a particular body type. A woman friend of Dragu's frequents strip clubs because she likes what she calls the "sex-filled atmosphere." She carries away with her a rich store of visual memories that continue to inspire her. She describes one stripper she will never forget.

"She was on her knees on the floor and she was wearing a black halter top and there were strobe lights. She was pulsating up and down on her knees, with her hands at her breasts and her head thrown back. It was incredibly passionate, and I was totally knocked out, and I can remember this image still."

I myself will never forget a woman who performed one evening when I was out watching strippers with Dragu. She was pretty in a conventional way, but there was also something lusty about her that gave some life to her prettiness. There came a moment in her show when she began to crawl across the stage on her hands and knees. It was a circular stage in the centre of the room. She was crawling away from me, moving slowly but with intense deliberation towards a cluster of men directly opposite where I sat. I could see the eyes of those men as they watched her approach, and amazingly, although I was watching her from behind, I found her movement across the stage as riveting as they did. It was a slow, passionate dance enacted on hands and knees. It held so much power and intensity that the whole roomful of people became alert during the moments it took.

Art is usually identified by form rather than content. There are certain established art forms: painting, sculpture, dance, music, acting. If the product is unsatisfying, it does not cease to be art, but is simply regarded as bad art. Thus, it is not the fact that stripping is often bad that makes it a non art. The reason stripping is not art is that its sexual focus disqualifies it. The sex in stripping is thought to be more real than representational. The theatrical basis of stripping is seen as a mere device in what is essentially a sexual service.

Actually, stripping is a game of catch between fact and fiction, between reality and representation, and it rides the line between life and theatre in a unique way. Yet it is a theatrical form, as valid as any other theatrical form. General expectation may keep it in a crude state, but it has the potential to transcend the limitations we impose on it.

When Dragu first began stripping, she had a set of ideas that was unusual, but not totally anomalous among strippers. Her job, as she saw it, was to express the God-spirit innate in sexuality. She wanted to transcend the gutter image of stripping with the power of her belief that sex is holy and that its holiness can be artistically represented through the medium of performance. This was her challenge as she saw it at the age of twenty. Though young, she was fairly well-equipped to attempt it. She had spent her teenage years training and performing with a small modern dance company based in Calgary. At 18, she went to New York to extend her dance skills. By the time she arrived in Montreal and started her first stripping job, she was a seasoned performer and choreographer.

Dragu's enthusiasm for stripping was also an asset. She loved to dance and perform – she is, in fact, one of those people who is more comfortable on stage than off – so she was thrilled to be paid money to put on a show six times a night for a live audience.

She did well at first. There were evenings when Dragu danced and the club grew hushed, and afterward, the waiter said to her: "When you dance, this place is like a church." He told her he got bigger tips on the nights she worked. Men sent her notes. One from a regular said: "You become more amazing every day." Some sent flowers. Once when she was doing a slow, sad striptease she noticed a man sitting with his buddies, watching her and silently crying. After her show he called her name in a quiet voice and she turned to look at him. He stood up and said "merci," and touched his fingertips to his lips, then turned and left the club.

Another time a man walked up to the stage as she finished her set and threw his gloves at her feet. She says she felt like an evangelist with a convert come forth to be blessed. The club grew still and everyone waited to see what would happen. Dragu didn't know what to do. There was nothing explicit in the man's gesture. She and he stared at each other until he said at last: "Everything is so sensuous

I can't stand it," and covered his face with his hands. His buddies retrieved the gloves and led him away.

But there was, of course, plenty of weird and negative feedback too, and it chipped away at her enthusiasm, until eventually she began to feel overwhelmed by the very morality she had set out to conquer.

At the end of her second year as a stripper, Dragu became involved in making a documentary film about stripping. At her insistence, the director agreed to shoot one dance scene in a church. Dragu picked out a beautiful Anglican church in the neighbourhood where she lived, and got permission from the minister to film a classical dance sequence for a fantasy scene. The sequence did not involve stripping, but Dragu felt guilty that she hadn't told the minister what the film was about. She worried that he might get into trouble if his church was recognized. Finally, she went to see him and confessed that she was a stripper and that the film was about stripping. She explained that she wanted to do the church scene for a part of the film in which she talked about the spiritual work of strippers. She told him her idea that strippers relieve sexual and spiritual pain.

The minister didn't patronize her, which is what she expected. He told her that she had found a special calling, and that the altar of God existed in unexpected places, even nightclubs. Dragu felt sanctioned. But this victory marked the end of her belief that she could change the world through spiritually-based representations of sexuality. She had come to doubt the integrity of her vision. Despite the occasional triumph, she was more and more affected by the disdain of most of the world for her and her job. In the end, her fall from grace was profound, and she experienced a terrible erosion of her values and her belief in herself.

It is difficult to find the right perspective on this period of Dragu's career. What she was doing could be seen as a naive attempt to persuade men in particular and the world in general to think of sex as a holy force. This amounts to nothing less than trying to shake the Christian-Judaic foundations of society with a combination of spiritual conviction and performance skill. But in another way, she was attempting something more realistic and specific, and that was to bring art, in its most sublime sense, into the strip club. If this was her purpose, she did have some success – at times stirring in her audience a genuine sense of awe. But her understanding of stripping was unique within the prevailing mass vision, and finding just a few people who shared her vision was not enough to sustain her.

Dragu's disenchantment caused her to move from an inspirational to a dramatic mode of stripping. She began to satirize audience views of women and sex, to dramatize her hostile feelings towards men, and to abstract her own spiritual-sexual dilemma. She did a striptease in which she portrayed a mechanical doll with a fixed smile, and she did some S&M acts using whips and toy guns. In one of her shows she came out dressed as a preacher beating a tambourine, and stripped to reveal a vulnerable woman in a torn dress. Her message was the same, but she had now begun to focus on its negative aspects.

Dragu is not alone in her desire to portray the spiritual and transcendent aspects of sexuality. Among the many strippers I have seen are a few who have affected me in a profound way. Morgana was one of these. I saw her at Le Strip – the Toronto club that is set up like a theatre and doesn't serve liquor. Morgana did an extended spread show. That is, following a very minimal dance, she sat down on a chair facing the audience, spread her legs, and rotated her pelvis. She moved her chair to different parts of the stage to offer each section of the audience a close view of her revolving vulva, and she maintained intense eye contact with her audience throughout.

It's difficult to know exactly what made the show extraordinary. I myself was transfixed. Genitalia does have a certain visual potency all its own, but it was Morgana's presence above all that was compelling. She projected serenity, intelligence and compassion as well as warmth and sensuality. She seemed to be present with her whole being to what she was doing. I suppose it was the juxtaposition of the enlightened with the sexual, and the way that both seemed to exist as absolutes, that lifted Morgana's work into the realm of the sublime. After the show, several men stood up to shake her hand as she came through the crowd on her way to the dressing room. It appeared that one old man had come solely for Morgana's show – he left right after it, pausing at the back of the room to salute and shout: "That's the real Morgana!" The overwhelming consensus of respect and admiration was perhaps unusual for a strip club, but entirely appropriate.

Learning afterwards something about Morgana's politics and sensibilities, I felt I had not misread her. What she thinks about g-strings is that strippers should not have to wear them. To make a negotiable piece of merchandise out of a woman's crotch is, she believes, the ultimate in objectification, and immoral. Her vision as a stripper is to make men aware of greater possibilities in their relationships with women by showing them how much a woman can enjoy herself sexually. Morgana describes herself as political, emotional and practical rather than spiritual, and yet her quest seems very close to the one Dragu pursued in her early stripping years.

Dragu claims that many strippers deny the spiritual element of their performances. Denese, for example.

But I was there when it happened, says Dragu. *It's like being at a prayer meeting when everyone is speaking in tongues, and then afterwards, they forget.*

Denese was dancing in the basement bar of the Colonial Tavern. She wasn't allowed to work upstairs because she is black. It was the pits in the basement – the clientele was mostly drunks who had wandered in off Yonge Street. Everybody hated working down there.

She came out wearing a black and white caftan with a hood, and carrying a rose – very unusual getup for a stripper. She looked like a strange, black clown. She crept around the stage in a concentrated, alert way, as if she were circling the campfire, listening to sounds that nobody else could hear. I felt right from the start of her dance that something was going to happen, though I didn't know what.

She stripped down to a leotard. Workout clothes have become sexy since then, but they weren't thought of that way in the seventies. Besides that, she had her hair in a very short afro. She is quite beautiful and she looked good, but her style was definitely not stripperesque. However, she was very aware of the challenge of her aesthetic and aware of her position in the club as a black woman. She wanted to be very black.

Her dance started off slow and got faster and hotter. No bumps and grinds, but lots of kicks and spins and arm slashing – a combination of athletics, jazz dance and Graham dance. You have to be technically very good to do what she did, but it wasn't just that she was technically good. A kind of joy swept through her, and although there was hardly anybody watching her, she pushed herself through incredible energy and dynamics till she was dripping and gleaming with sweat. She seemed to glow. She was proud and strong and yet she wasn't filled with hatred. Her strength was a kind of joy, a joy of the body and the soul. She was pure, transcendent energy.

The idea that numenous art might exist in a strip club is a new one on many people. But there are those who visit clubs specifically in search of God experience. Some of these people describe the best strippers as the ones who "strip to the soul." A man Dragu interviewed in Miami told her that strippers make him feel "at peace." A woman who put herself through school working as a waitress in strip clubs amazed me one day when she said about clubs:

"You need truths. That's the only place I can find peace."

Paul, the writer, who is introduced in "Getting Down with the Boys," thinks that striptease offers a special context that makes transcendent experience possible. This special context, he believes, is the combination of performance and nakedness. In the stripper's case, the performer's figurative nudity becomes a factual, naked truth, and when combined with the projection by the stripper of a strong inner being, the result is truly overwhelming.

Stripping embraces both the ritual and the creative, moving between a religious and an artistic expression of sexuality. In one sense it is a formal sexual rite with a fixed sequence – an official performance given by one sex for the other. But it is also a forum for the stripper's individual portrayal of sexuality. Stripping has many shortcomings with respect to both of these functions, yet it is one of the few shrines that exists in our culture for the representation of sexuality.

Glossary

Every job has its lingo. Stripper lingo is a fabulous combination of a Raymond Chandler movie and showbiz talk. Here is a random sampling of some important terms that are temporarily popular.

Working for the House *was the first term I learned as a stripper, on the rue Ste. Catherine in Montreal. I was excited about my new job, but a greenhorn. Dancing, costumes and customers were all good, but within my first week after refusing any drink except orange juice, the bartender – a wrinkle-faced ex truck driver kind of guy in a rumpled short-sleeved white shirt and black bow tie – cautiously looked both ways and nodded me over to the bar. He leaned over and said, "You – you don't work for the house? Lissen, kid. Wha d'ya think pays your salary? We're open to sell liquor. No cover at the door – customers gotta buy booze. If they wanna buy you a drink, say yes thank you and order a screwdriver with the orange juice on the side. If you don't want the vodka, give it to one of the other girls or dump it in the plants – don't let the customer catchya. And when you get the drink, wave at him and smile." His eyes raised hopefully, appraised me, and then dismissed me as he went to fill* *orders. A couple of days later, as he delivered me my fiftieth screwdriver and I smilingly raised my glass to a boyish business executive, the bartender said warmly, "You're not a bad kid." I discreetly tossed the vodka into a plant and sipped my o.j. That's working for the house!*

Folks who don't work in bars usually say: What a terrible waste of liquor. Why didn't he just give you the orange juice, charge for the liquor and you and he could pocket the profits. That deal is one of many **Scams** *(ways to make money illegally), and liquor scams are dangerous for the bartender, who stands to lose both his job and his licence. 99% of bartenders don't mess around. Stocktaking (a way the manager keeps on eye on liquor quantities and sales), inspections by the licensing commission, complaints from customers and snitches from co-workers all help to keep the bartender straight. But there are many ways for a bartender to make extra money, should he care to try, especially with the help of waitresses, strippers or* **B-girls**.

I guess the B stands for Bar or Booze or just plain Bad. In wartime, according to the movies, soldiers are warned off B-girls (That club is off limits to army personnel.) Besides soldiers, favourite **Marks** *(patsies) include logging camp, mining camp and construction camp workers who toil for six months up north and then come to town to spend their earnings. Also tourists and travelling businessmen who are feeling lonely. A B-girl offers company and conversation if the mark is paying for her drinks. She could be drinking the real thing, which makes her relatively legal, or she could be consuming* **Watered Down Drinks**.

These contain just enough liquor to make the drink smell like liquor so the mark doesn't get wise to the scam. But if she's drinking straight soda water or coca cola without a drop of liquor in it, she can really **Fleece** *a customer fast, and she can work all night without getting drunk. Another scam which is harder is selling* **Unmarked Liquor**. *To keep track of it, the bartender runs it through just one or two girls and their customers.*

The most famous B-girl scam is the **Champagne Hustle**. *This is a very old two-step and is practised from Berlin to Paris to New York to Atlantic City. One or two girls sit at a mark's table and ask if he wants some company and if he would buy them a drink. But the drink they want is champagne. The joints that go in for this scam stock a lot of champagne, and some charge champagne prices for all* *drinks, so you might as well.*

Illegal scams are all about making ***Easy Money****. Easy money is a state of mind, the essence of capitalism, a carrot at the end of a string, a hustle, a good idea, a get-rich-quick concept or, more broadly, it means that while civilians are working in offices and factories, we strippers (or hookers, or bartenders) are making money in a social industry. We are in an atmosphere of play. We are working in the place where civilian folks come to spend the money they earn at straight jobs.*

Nightlife puts you in contact with all kinds of nightlife types, for instance, ***Rounders****, who are petty crooks involved in small crimes like B&E's, shoplifting, fencing, hooking, pimping, numbers rackets and bookmaking. Rounders feel comfortable in bars and use them as places to meet and relax between shifts. And often where there are rounders, there are on-duty and off-duty* ***Cops****.*

Well, that's the Raymond Chandler side of stripper lingo. Here is the burlesque side of it.

My favourite term is ***Flashing*** *because it makes me think of dirty old men. It means stretching your g-string to offer the audience a glimpse of pubic hair. This is a tease in g-string off areas, but it is all you get in g-string on areas.*

A ***Floor Show*** *is a lying-down dance that is more or less a mime of having sex with an invisible partner. You tease by opening and closing your legs, stretch, kick, roll over and generally romp about on your back, your belly or your knees. Floor shows are the climax of a strip act. They can be funny, irreverent, sad, touching, romantic, hot, psychedelic or athletic. They come in as many versions as there are strippers.*

Spread Shows *are more explicit. If you're working in a place that allows the g-string to come off, you can do a spread show, which involves opening up your legs and letting the customers look right in there.*

If you do your spread show or floor show on a customer's table, it is called ***Working the Tables****. I used to know a stripper called Cindy who was exceptional at this. She would pick a table of big spenders, hop up on the table and move the drinks and ashtrays out of the way. She kneeled and arched backwards till her head touched the table top. The men slipped money into her g-string till it was loaded down like a fluffy tutu.*

The unspoken but (usually) well understood rule is that men can tip but not touch. Part of the ritual is that the stripper lifts the g-string elastic so the men don't touch her at all, except vicariously, with their money.

Table Dancing *is different than working the tables. For this, you carry around a wooden or plexiglass box about the size of a milk crate. Customers who want you will call you and your box over to their table where you get up on the box and dance just for them. They pay you directly. In some places there is a flat rate, like five dollars, but some clubs work out a sliding scale for touching privileges – five dollars to touch a thigh, ten dollars for a breast, etc. At clubs that offer table dancing it is the strippers who do it – between sets – but table dancing is not stripping, at least not in my book.*

Bibliography

THE STRIPTEASE ESTABLISHMENT

Bibliography

Ann Corio, with Joseph Dimona, *This Was Burlesque* (New York: Grosset & Dunlap, 1968)
Ken Johnstone, "Salute to a stripper," *Maclean's*, October 20, 1962
Fonda Peters, Authors' Interview, Montreal, 1981

Notes

Luridness vs innocence: Corio, throughout
Josephine: Johnstone
Voluptuous vs toylike: Peters, pp. 2-3

WHY QUEEN ELIZABETH DOESN'T STRIP

Bibliography

John Cosway, "Nude Show Barely Fails to Take Off," *Toronto Sun*, Aug. 17, 1981

Jane Crockett, "Stripping Bit of a Grind," *Sunday Sun*, Toronto, Oct. 7, 1979
Ronald Evans, "You Can Stop Shaking," *Telegram*, Toronto, Sept. 20, 1961
Adele Freedman, "Margaret Dragu: Honky Tonk Philosopher Queen," *Fanfare, The Globe and Mail*, Toronto, June 14, 1978
Jerry Gladman, "Sexy Stella's in a twirl," *Sunday Sun*, Toronto, Oct. 25, 1981
Jerry Gladman, "Stripper's Road Paved with Bumps and Grinds," *Toronto Sun*, Nov. 6, 1981
Ken Johnstone, "Salute to a stripper," *Maclean's*, Oct. 20, 1962
John Keasler, "Glamour Gone-Gone from Go-Go in the Buff," *Miami News*, Jan. 10, 1979
William Littler, "Danceworks menu hardly traditional," *Toronto Star*, April 16, 1982
"Her Majesty the Queen vs. Bridget," Old City Hall, Toronto, March 22, 1979, Trial Transcript
Misty, *Strip* (Toronto: New Press, 1973)
"O-o-o-ps! Not in Kamloops, toots!," *Toronto Sun*, Jan. 14, 1982
Martin Ralbovsky, "Nude Beauty Threatens Different Kind of Suit," *Miami News*, Nov. 13, 1979
"Beverly Hills Bar to Bump 'n' Grind to Halt," *Sunday Star*, Toronto, April 4, 1982
Sharon Steeves, "Etobicoke gunning for strip clubs," *Toronto Sun*, Sept. 21, 1982
"Strip Shakedown?" (source unknown), Miami, Dec. 17, 1959
"Strippers Inciting, Not Just Delighting," *Toronto Sun*, Aug. 27, 1981
Barbara Yaffe, "...and the strippers," *The Globe and Mail*, Toronto, May 23, 1982

Notes

University of bump 'n' grind: Littler
Enterprising tavern owner: Strippers Inciting
Not substantially moral: Steeves
St. John's first strip club: Yaffe
Oh come now: Misty, p. 77
Article on Dragu: Freedman
Josephine: Johnstone
Actress who posed nude: Gladman
Bridget's trial: Her Majesty

REVELATIONS

Bibliography

Flugel, J.C., *The Psychology of Clothes* (New York: International Universities Press Inc., 1930)
Laver, James, *Modesty in Dress* (London: William Heinemann Ltd., 1969)
Sobel, Bernard, *Burleycue* (NewYork: Farrar & Rinehart, 1931)
Gernsheim, Alison, *Victorian and Edwardian Fashion: A Photographic Survey* (New York: Dover Publications, Inc., 1981)

Notes

List of women's garments: Gernsheim, throughout
Leg as *limb* or *jambe*: Flugel, p. 66
Queen of Spain: Flugel, p. 66
Uproar caused by legs: Sobel, throughout
Stones thrown at bloomer wearers: Gernsheim, p. 81
Old gentlemen faint with emotion: Laver, p. 97

VICE

Bibliography

"Comedy act could cost lounge its license [sic]," *Toronto Star*, Oct. 30, 1974
Commandant De Grâce, Morality Division, Montreal Police, Authors' Interview, 1981
Claude Jaget, ed., *Prostitutes: Our Life* (Bristol, Eng: Falling Wall Press, 1980)
"Liquor board erred as censor: judges," *Toronto Star*, July 22, 1975
"LLBO blacklists MacLean team," *Globe & Mail,* Toronto, Oct. 30, 1979
"LLBO inspectors didn't have authority to interfere with club act, court rules," *Globe & Mail*, Toronto, July 22, 1975
John Massey on his talks with Berlin & Paris police, Authors' Interview, Toronto, 1981
Fonda Peters, Authors' Interview, Montreal, 1981
Acting Inspector Roberts, Morality Division, Vancouver Police, Authors' Interview, 1981
Michael Walsh, Authors' Interview, Vancouver, 1981

Notes

The Game:
Like a kid in school: De Grâce, pp. 2-3
Prostitutes: De Grâce, throughout
Cutting edge: Walsh, p.14
German morality: Massey, p.1
Federal law on nudity: Criminal Code of Canada, Sections 170:1 and 170:2
Montreal bylaw on mingling: No. 3416
Toronto bylaw on g-strings: No. 107-78:24(2)
MacLean and MacLean: *Globe* & *Star*
B.C. liquor board: Roberts, p.7

Vice in Montreal:
Quotes & opinions of De Grâce & assistant: De Grâce, throughout
French prostitutes' strike: Jaget, p.45
Morality the lowest plane of existence: Peters, p.14
The police would come into the club: Peters, p.14
Difficult to say no: Peters, p.14

Vice in Vancouver:
Quotes & opinions of Acting Inspector Roberts: Roberts throughout

THE COCK'S DANCE

Bibliography

"Safe, sexy thrills," *Self*, January 1981
"A Horse of a Different Gender," *Miami News*, March 14, 1975
"Girls' Night Out," *Miami Herald*, August 26, 1979
"Stage Equality," *Miami Herald*, August 26, 1979
"Etobicoke gunning for strip clubs," *Toronto Sun*, September 21, 1982
"Strippers inciting, not just delighting," *Toronto Sun*, August 27, 1981
Alan Stewart, "Those boys who bump and grind," *Toronto Star*, (date unknown) 1981
Richard Wortley, *A Pictorial History of Striptease* (London: Octopus Books Ltd., 1976)
Jason Eros, Authors' Interview, Toronto, 1983

Notes

Bonding, church, safe and guilt free: *Self*
Way to get out of the house: *Miami News*
Laughs and a good time: *Miami Herald* (Girls)
Cute, crazy and fun: *Miami Herald* (Stage)
Immoral: *Toronto Sun* (Gunning)
Disgusting & disgraceful: *Toronto Sun* (Inciting)
Sleazy & contemptible: Stewart
Boring: Wortley
Polish teenage girls: Jason, p. 11
Getting head: Jason, pp. 13-14
Men in control: Stewart

HONOUR & JEALOUSY

Bibliography

Bridget, Authors' Interview, Toronto, 1981
Gwendolyn, Authors' Interview, Toronto, 1981
Desirée, Authors' Interview, Toronto, 1981
Fonda Peters, Authors' Interview, Montreal, 1981
Zaide, Authors' Interview, Toronto, 1981

Notes

The stories and comments of the above-mentioned are taken from their respective interviews.

THE STRIPPER AND THE GANGSTER

Bibliography

CBC/Norfolk Communications, *Connections*, June 1977 & March 1979
Debbie, Authors' Interview, Montreal, 1981

"Devant la CECO," *La presse* (date unknown)
Gwendolyn, Authors' Interview, Toronto, 1981
Georges Simenon, *Maigret Loses His Temper* (New York/London: Harcourt Brace Jovanovich, 1980)
Fonda Peters, Authors' Interview, Montreal, 1981
"Treize meurtres," *La presse*, January 21, 1975
Zaide, Authors' Interview, Toronto, 1981

Notes

Headlines: from the collection of Centre documentation de *La presse*, 1975 & 1976
Maigret: Simenon, p.36
Gargantua: *La presse* (Jan. 21/75)
Connections: CBC/Norfolk
Zaide's story: Zaide, p.13
Debbie's story: Debbie, pp. 9-10
Denise testifies: *La presse* (unknown)
Gwendolyn's Denise: Gwendolyn, p.24
Fonda's Denise: Fonda, p.22

GETTING DOWN WITH THE BOYS

Bibliography

Bridget, Authors' Interview, Toronto, 1981
Carl, Authors' Interview, Vancouver, 1981
Clive, Authors' Interview, Toronto, 1982
Debbie, Authors' Interview, Montreal, 1981
Denese, Authors' Interview, Toronto, 1981
Gilles, Authors' Interview, Toronto, 1981
Gwendolyn, Authors' Interview, Toronto, 1981
Fonda Peters, Author's Interview, Montreal, 1981
Jack, Authors' Interview, Toronto, 1981
Jamie, Authors' Interview, Vancouver, 1981
Jeannie, Authors' Interview, Montreal, 1981
Matt, Authors' Interview, Toronto, 1983
Morgana, Authors' Interview, Toronto, 1981
Paul, Authors' Interview, Toronto, 1984

Ralph, Authors' Interview, Toronto, 1982

Notes

The opinions and comments of the above-mentioned are taken from their respective interviews.

AT THE SHRINE OF THE STRIPPER

Bibliography

Elizabeth, Authors' Interview, 1981
Guatemala man, Authors' Interview, 1981
James Laver, *Modesty in Dress* (London: William Heinemann Ltd., 1969)
"Her Majesty the Queen vs. Bridget," Old City Hall, Toronto, March 22, 1979, Trial Transcript
Morgana, Authors' Interview, Toronto, 1981
Paul, Authors' Interview, Toronto, 1984
Janet Walczewski, director, *Theatre for Strangers*, Daro Productions
Michael Walsh, Authors' Interview, Vancouver, 1981
Wendy, Conversation Notes, Toronto, 1982

Notes

Diana preparing for the chase: Laver, p.104
Bridget no ballet: Her Majesty, p.24
Legal secretary strip story: Walsh, p.11
Sex-filled atmosphere: Elizabeth, p.1
Stripper in black halter top: Elizabeth, p.3
Documentary film about stripping: Walczewski
Morgana's views: Morgana, throughout
At peace: Guatemala man, p.1
You need truths: Wendy
Transcendence: Paul, throughout

Books

Books on Stripping and Sexuality

Alexander, H.M., *Strip Tease: The Vanquished Art of Burlesque* (New York: Knight Publishers, 1938)

Baker, Josephine and Bouillon, Jo, *Josephine*, translated by Mariana Fitzpatrick (New York: Harper & Row, 1977)

Barber, Rowland, *The Night They Raided Minsky's* (New York: Simon and Schuster, 1960)

Bolton, Guy, *Bring On The Girls* (New York: Simon and Schuster, 1953)

Bruce, Honey, *Honey: The Life And Loves Of Lenny's Shady Lady* (Chicago: Playboy Press, 1978)

Brusse, Jan, *Nights In Paris*, translated by Arthur H. Whitney, photographs by Daniel Frasnay (London: André Deutsch Ltd., 1958)

Chernin, Kim, *The Obsession: Reflections On The Tyranny Of Slenderness* (New York: Harper Colophon Books, 1981)

Corio, Ann, with Dimona, Joseph, *This Was Burlesque* (New York: Grosset & Dunlap, 1968)

Flugel, J.C., *The Psychology Of Clothes* (New York: International Universities Press, Inc., 1930)

Friday, Nancy, *Men In Love* (New York: Dell Publishing Co. Ltd., 1980)

Hammond, Paul, *French Undressing: Naughty Postcards From 1900 to 1920* (London: Jupiter Books, 1974)

Hammond, Percy, *But Is It Art?* (New York: Doubleday, 1927)

Jaget, Claude, ed., *Prostitutes: Our Life* (Bristol, Eng.: Falling Wall Press, 1980)

Laver, James, *Modesty In Dress* (London: William Heinemann Ltd., 1969)

Lee, Gypsy Rose, *A Memoir* (New York: Harper & Bros., 1957)

Meiselas, Susan, *Carnival Strippers* (New York: Farrar, Straus and Giroux, 1976)

Misty, *Strip* (Toronto: New Press, 1973)

Sobel, Bernard, *Burleycue* (New York: Farrar & Rinehart, 1931)

Wortley, Richard, *A Pictorial History Of Striptease* (London: Octopus Books Ltd., 1976)

Zeidman, Irving, *The American Burlesque Show* (New York: Hawthorn Books, Inc., 1967)

Margaret Dragu A.S.A. Harrison
(photo by John Massey)

Born in Toronto in 1948, A.S.A. Harrison co-authored two porn novels at an early age, and went on to publish a series of interviews with women titled *Orgasms*. She has written articles and fiction for numerous mainstream and literary publications.

Margaret Dragu was born in Regina in 1953. She has enjoyed a long career as a performance artist and choreographer, presenting her work internationally in many venues, including theatres, art galleries and museums. She is also a writer, filmmaker, and video artist.

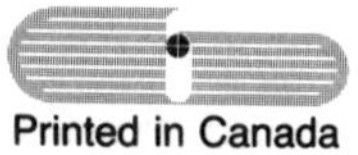

Printed in Canada